P. EUGENE POULIN

THE HOLY VIRGIN'S HOUSE

THE TRUE STORY OF ITS DISCOVERY

Compiled by
P. Philibert De La Chaise
1980-1985

Translated by
Ivi Richichi
1999

Editor
Georgina Özer

arıkan yayınları

Taşsavaklar Sokak No:10 34410 Cağaloğlu / İstanbul / Türkiye
Tel.: (0212) 522 22 23 - 520 18 92   Fax.: (0212) 513 40 44
web site: www.holyvirginhouse.com
E-mail: sales@holyvirginhouse.com

© Arıkan Yayınları Tic. San. Ltd. Şti. - 1999

First Edition: İstanbul, 1999
ISBN: 975-7305-28-6

Printing: OMAŞ® Ofset A.Ş.

We are honoured to present this work, which has never been published.

We thank Mgr. Giuseppe Bernardini and the Christian community of Izmir, who informed us of its existence.

CONTENTS

Author of the Journal, Rev. P. Eugene Poulin (Alias Gabrielovich)
1843-1928

J.M.J.   History of Panaghi Capouli 1905

Monument erected to the glory of the Blessed Virgin

In nomine Domini - Amen

Note to the reader:

Since the beginning we have carefully written everyday facts and events concerning Panaghia Capouli; it is according to these written documents and facts, that I, a constant witness from the beginning until the present date, write this history.

Therefore, there is every guarantee of accuracy:

This is the reality.

If the text is not well written, it is my fault; please forgive me, and, bearing in mind only my good will and intention, pray for me.

Smyrna, House of Sacré Coeur

Wednesday. 5th February 1905

Gabrielovich (alias Father Poulin)

Curriculum Vitae of the Reverend Father Eug. Poulin, Lazarist
(Alias Gabrielovich 1843-1928)

Selection of the Annals, Mission of the Fraternity (Lazarists)

SMYRNA (İzmir) Turkey

M. Eugene Poulin

M.Eugene Poulin died on the night of 7 to 8 March, 1928.

He passed away in the Lord's peace aged eighty five, and after sixty three years of his religious vocation.

The day before his death the doctor had found him in good health. Auscultation had been quite good, giving no reason for anxiety. At about nine o'clock, he was sleeping peacefully. The next day he was lying in the same position, but he did not wake up.

M.Eugene Poulin was born on 4th July 1813 at Montillot, near Vezealy (Yonne). After a detailed study of the classics at the small seminary of Sens, he entered the great seminary, and later Saint Lazare (6th October 1865).

He was ordained on 15th June 1857.

He was a missionary for a while at Gregy (Brie), later he entered the little seminary of Saint-Leger (Soissons), and finally, Saint-Benoit (Constantinople) in 1873. He held office as Procurator Director of the College, Provincial procurator, Cathechiser at the Orphanage of Tchokour-Bostan.

For a while he was designated to Montpellier (1887). There he remained for a short time, before leaving for Izmir, where he had been appointed as Superior.

"I'll not stay at Izmir even for six months", objected the Reverend Father, giving the debilitating hot season as a pretext.

He remained for thirty-nine years.

Favouring strict discipline, he applied it wisely, looking around him and observing for one long year, thinking things over and over before changing anything.

An intrepid defender of classic studies, he opposed the adoption of the modern system, even jeopardising the college's prosperity. The small number did not deter him. "Not the quantity but the quality," he used to say. This was good reason to empty a house. In 1903, the nomination of M.Deroo as director was considered necessary to increase student numbers. M.Poulin allowed this to happen, but regretted bitterly the decline of his dear Latin language.

He was a priest not only at the altar, but everywhere. He possessed a spirit of faith and piety, strong faith, above all simplicity with a mysticism that was entirely interior. His tenacity in prayer impressed everybody. Afflicted with a stammer, he tried hard to pronounce a word well, repeating it over and over, even though this tired his listeners.

In spite of being Director of the college and ministering to our nuns- which he did until the end- he a found time for leisure: This leisure time was filled by two kinds of work, which he did with the obstinacy of an ox, without looking around him and with considerable feeling, I dare say; just finding his path, deep and straight.

It is well known that studies of Panaghia Capouli (for there are more than two thick books unpublished) have been printed.

They comprise five small books or volumes, signed Gabrielovich, a nickname derived from Gabriel, his father's christian name. [1]

---

[1] Panaghia Capouli or the Holy Virgin's House, near Efesus; Efesus or Jerusalem, the grave of the Holy Virgin, not Sion or Gethsemane. A last word about the place where the Holy Virgin died.

They are studies of real value, although their impact may be lessened because of the writer's trenchant means of expression, his combative stance, which disturb the reader. But once the first impression had been overcome and upon carefully reading the proofs, it was decided that the thesis concerning Efesus was not an invention of C. Emmerich.

Even though M. Poulin had no universitary diploma, he did not hesitate to argue with the most eminent scholars. He wrote many letters to F. Lagrange, to Mgr. Duchesne and other prominent scholars.

He fought until the end, reading his own writings again and again to correct or to add something, convinced that he was right. His adversaries kept silent because they could find nothing to object to.

For many years M. Poulin lived in solitude. Some elderly nuns and very rare friends came to visit him from time to time.

But he was not forgotten: this was obvious on the day of his funeral.

The church of Saint Polycarpe, in spite of it being so inaccessible, -because it is surrounded by ruins- was full of gentlemen, most of them notables who wished to honour him by paying their last respects to a man whose name had filled all their youth, their years at the college and had brought back their best memories.

The best way to end this short note is to point out the obituary published in the modest "Communication" by the Archbishop of Smyrna: "He arouses in the heart of everyone who has known him, and in the youth of Smyrna whom he has brought up a deep and unforgettable feeling of tenderness, admiration and gratitude."

The Holy Virgin died at Efesus. The first text remains as yet discovered.

Chapter I

How did the idea of research come about?

Nobody among us had ever heard of the Panaghia, the house, the grave; nobody, absolutely nobody.

M. Vincent didn't think so, neither did M. Portal.

In mid- November 1890, Sister Mairet, Superior of the Providence, asked me for a book to read in the refectory.

"Of course, Sister" said I. I went to the Library, climbed up a ladder, got some books and brought them to my room, to see which was the best for her. I put them in order, and started looking at them one by one. There was an old in-octavo bound in sheepskin, in bad condition. I had taken it without noticing it among the other books.

Reading the title-page, I felt a surge of eagerness. "What is it doing here? After twenty years it is here to borrow me!"

To understand my exlamation, my eagerness, we must go back to 1868-69.

I was then a young priest about 25 years old, at Gregy, near Melun, with M. de Lesquen and M. Blot under the leadership of the Venerable Father Denys, former Superior of the Great Seminary at Carcassonne (Evreux), who also bore the title of Visiteur of Province de France and Superior of Gregy. The good Father Denys was very pious and very devoted to mystic studies. I still remember how, with a childish faith, he spoke to us during evening recreation about his favourite reading matter; Catherine Emmerich, Marie d'Agreda etc.etc.

As much as the good old man had a naive trust and esteem for these prophets, we youngsters and particularly I, did not have any esteem for these "women visionaries". We laughed so much at the joyful jokes we made every time the holy man brought up the subject he cherished so much.

It had not been a momentary impression, it had been a forgone conclusion. In fact for twenty years I never believed a single one of the visionaries;

I believed that I would be demeaned reading only one page of Marie d'Agreda or Catherine Emmerich or Sainte Gertrude or indeed any of them.

Many people had shared these feelings and they still do. I was of the same opinion until November 1890, when my eyes glanced over the old in-octavo. I read:

"The Suffering Passion of Jesus Christ, according to Catherine Emmerich's Visions."

As one could imagine, the book was quickly removed from the pile of other books, and disdainfully put aside on my table. I kept on looking at the other books.

My choice completed, I gathered up the other books and took them back to the Library. A day later, what was my surprise when I saw the book so disdainfully thrown aside the day before; it was on my table in the same place.

"That is strange: how could I have forgotten it yesterday? However, the book is thick and quite visible....but that's enough: I have some other books for the library that I'll take it back with.

The next day, "The Suffering Passion" of C. Emmerich was still on my table: Nevertheless it seemed that I had taken it back to the Library!.. Of course... I had intended to, but I had not done so....

It was the same .. the following day, and for the next 2-3 days. "Is this book making fun of me?" Finally I threw the book violently into the corner of the room, where it fell with its pages open and broken in two. Well done! Stay there and do not annoy me any more".

One week had passed, the book was still on the floor, in the same place, in the same position. I laughed every time and felt in myself a childish revenge every time I saw it. I ask your pardon, reader, for all these personal details that I am supposed to only know myself, but as we shall see later, from the very beginning they have obviously revealed the fact of which we will have the proof afterwards. One should be aware that many times we are guided more often than we guide.

This is a sign of providence, a sign which tells us a lot; it suggests we have the trust to finish a task and also gives us the necessary courage to go forward. Could it be understood why I spent one week in front of the book that was so hateful, that seemed of so little value without any thought of picking it up to see what it was about?

Strangely, the man who cleans my room didn't pick it up or put it elsewhere. ....oh! no.. I don't say miraculous, it is strange, extraordinary. One morning, on coming back into my room as usual at about six o'clock after morning prayers, I had a look at the unfortunate book; my blood pounded in my veins, a reflexion came into my mind. "Really it is neither wise nor right to be against a book without knowing it, to condemn it without having read it, either.

This reflection changed something in me. Was it not ridiculous that for twenty years I had ridiculed the book and the writings of C. Emmerich without having read a single line, without knowing who she was? To get the book I needed to take one step, but when I tried to open it a deadly aversion came over me. "Do open and read it", common sense was telling me but repugnance stopped me. I stood for about five or six minutes, the book in my hands, unable to decide. Had it been only "Passion" I could have read it easily, but for that epithet "suffering". The "suffering passion of Jesus Christ" was full of mysticism and this horrified me. After thinking hard I decided:

"I'll read a little, just to see who this Catherine Emmerich; is that doesn't engage me, I am not obliged to read the whole book."

This good decision taken, I opened the book. I was ashamed, I didn't wish to be seen with this book in my hands!... So I stood by the corner of the table ready to throw it down if somebody should knock on my door.

I read the foreword first... Let us go on!.. Then the preface, then the third.., a note concerning C. Emmerich. "Here we are!." I started to read this note slowly, looking for some stupidities or extravagances.

You can imagine my surprise!... It was something very pious, very simple, all conforming to good sense: I was astonished!. There was sweetness, words and style which invaded you slowly, going straight to your heart.

I was reading, charmed by the text when the big bell rang:

"What! Seven o'clock already!" I had been reading for one hour. I was thrilled. I put the book down open on my table and left for the church.

At eight o'clock I took up my book again, but this time I didn't hide.. I read the note on C. Emmerich until the end, with delight in everything I was reading and everything I was learning. But still I was far from being a convert.

Following the note there was a title in big black letters:

"The Suffering Passion of Jesus Christ according to C. Emmerich."

I looked at this title and all my repugnancy came back again. But this time I overcame it. I turned the page and I continued reading. I had never read anything so pious, so beautiful, so interesting about our Lord's Passion, except the Gospel. I wasn't reading.. I was just devouring the pages...

Should I keep for myself this beauty, this delight, this unexpected illumination?

I was in a hurry to share my discovery with my friends. But they didn't agree with me.. a loud sign of disagreement was their only answer to my proposition. Nonsense! said one of them. Sheer stupidity, said another..

"Girlish dreams," said a third.. "But do read it", I answered, "read and you will see"...."Me, reading things like that!" they replied "I have no time to waste!...

If I read it I must confess" said a fourth...and the jokes went on and everybody was laughing. I was alone against this opposition. In spite of my arguments, my exhortations, I couldn't convince them.

Since that moment, every evening or during recreation, or occasionally because of my reading, or because of some reflection, there were the most amicable arguments.

One evening, in December 1890 or January 1891..., we were arguing eagerly as always about C. Emmerich when one of our elders, fatherly M. Dubulle approached me and said: "M. Superior, I was, like you, unbelieving, and without any will to read, But then I read it and now I believe what it says".

"Oh! I don't believe it at all," said I quickly;" But I agree it is very simple, very pious, very right and very interesting."-Have you read the Holy Virgin's Life?" asked M. Dubulle.-" No. I don't know if it exists." "Would you like to read it?" - "Of course, with pleasure".

After this answer M. Dubulle left the community for his room, which was at the front, and came back holding a small book bound in black, titled:

"The Holy Mary's life according to the visions of C. Emmerich."

Translation from German by the Abbe Calzales, etc.

I took the book eagerly and started to read it with a delicious feeling: there was the same piety, the same simplicity, the same rectitude, the same attractive unction, the same interesting facts and sayings.

For some days it was the subject of new conversations and new arguments.

I was reading the last chapters, where the visionary speaks about Mary's stay at Efesus, her house, her death, her grave. "What is this?" I exclaimed- I had never thought in my life of Jerusalem or Efesus, or of Efesus more than of Jerusalem! I had never had the opportunity of any revelation! Meanwhile, the question was transformed and full of interest for us:

- We are at Smyrna, and thus interested in Efesus.

Thus, during first recreation I loudly exlaimed my discovery to all: "Heys all of you, listen, listen to me! I have found the answer!"

The discussions started again with more passion than before. For weeks, for months, it was the main subject of our conversations.

Meantime, by common agreement we adopted a resolution: "It is quite easy" one said. –"We can go and see if it is true or it isn't. If it is true we have to accept the evidence, if it is not true then we finish with C. Emmerich, she will be considered to be only a visionary, thus nobody will speak about her any more."

It was decided that we should go during the summer holiday. It was January, so we had six months before us, all the necessary time to quieten our spirits, to give mature consideration to the question and to be prepared seriously for this experience.

Meantime, two circumstances confirmed our decision.

M. Jung, an old non-commissioned officer, a professor of Holy Scriptures, of Hebrew, of natural sciences, of mathematics and therefore a teacher of science at the College of Sacré Coeur, was as much as for his personality, studies and education, also well known as being the most opposed to everything concerning mysticism, dreams and visions.

Thus, he was one of the adversaries of C.Emmerich, and one of the most implacable. He used to say: "Girls' dreams". For him the matter was finished. "But do read, do read:" - "Should I waste my time reading these absurdities? Am I supposed to sin!" and so on and so on. But one evening in March or April 1891 the porter brought a well wrapped packet.

"For M. Jung", he said. I brought the packet in without opening it:

"A packet for you, M. Jung". M. Jung knew in advance the contents of the packet. "Oh yes: I know what it is," he said, annoyed. "Thank you, put it there." What was the mysterious packet which annoyed Mr. Jung so much? We knew at once.

It seemed that Sister Grancey had been a passionate adherent of C. Emmerich. for a long time Thus, as she had often said, she had been looking for someone who would excavate the vicinities around Efesus, and try to find the House as well as the grave mentioned by C. Emmerich.

In those days M. Jung was in charge of celebrating the mass at the French Hospital (Hopital Français) every day in the morning.

He had the opportunity to speak to Sister Grancey about our discussions and soon she thought to herself: "I have found the right man!.."

They discussed the matter ....In the morning during breakfast M. Jung rejected everything as an unrelenting sceptic, and the Sister contested his opinions with all her heart; C. Emmerich's visions weren't nonsense, nor so ridiculous as he liked to believe... Finally, he was wrong to reject her ideas without knowing what they were!. "I'll send you the book" she said one day and in conclusion: "Do promise me you'll read it." The small packet was nothing other than the aforesaid book, sent by Sister Grancey....

M. Jung, in order to get rid of Sister Grancey, took the book at nine o'clock in the evening, after prayers, and before going to bed, he opened it and started reading... He read the first page, then the second, then the third and finally the whole book, to the last line. He read the whole night. "At four o'clock in the morning", he said, "I was still reading".

Like me, he was completely overwhelmed by the charm of the story.

Our conversation was now completely different "I don't know", he said afterwards to the brothers of the Confraternity. "I can declare nothing as to the veracity of C. Emmerich's visions, but what greatly surprises me is that I didn't hesitate to confirm that nothing in these visions contests the Gospel; also, they fit in perfectly with the Holy Scripture, on many points they complement marvellously the silence of the Gospel. He added:

"I don't understand how a poor country girl, always ill, naive and ignorant could find, could have said such beautiful, such wise, such strange things if her visions had not been true:"

M.Jung's conversion at that moment was far from complete, but it was obvious that a deep impression had been made on him. Everybody knew M. Jung's competence regarding the Holy Scripture, his knowledge of Jewish customs, of his great intelligence, but they also knew of his aversion, his instinctive horror concerning visions and visionaries. For so implacable an opponent to change all at once, even though not yet frankly partisan, but a convinced admirer of C. Emmerich, there must be very serious reasons. Since that date the number of his aversions had diminished. As for those who were firm in their opposition, they were more moderate and calmer in their contradictions.

Something more important than M. Jung's conversion, in fact very important for us, whose consequences had been notable in terms of the question before us to be resolved took place. It happened in the February before M. Jung's conversion. I want to speak about the active intervention of M. Lobry in the Efesus case. In the middle of February, 1891, he came from Constantinople to Smyrna on a private visit. Of course, they told him about what preoccupied all of us, about Efesus and the plan to go and see it during the long holiday. M. Lobry, like M. Jung and myself, was hostile to visionaries and visions.

"I saw", he was saying one day, "I saw miracles at Lourdes. I am ready to confirm they were miracles, however I don't believe:.."

That was his way of thinking and his disposition. How did he become interested in this question? I don't know. After twelve years it still remains a mystery to me.

The important thing is that he agreed with us and supported us in the researches we were to undertake.

"Take this," he said to M. Jung, to mean he supported his thought. "Here are 50 francs for the journey." While saying that, he gave M. Jung 50 francs from his pocket. I could see, I could hear but I could not believe my eyes or my ears.

M. Lobry! M. Lobry speaking like that? In that way? Had he believed C. Emmerich? I was completely overwhelmed; in spite of being a very frank admirer and believer in C. Emmerich, I still was sceptical. I was in this troubled condition between belief and disbelief but common sense refused resolutely to accept it because substantial and convincing proof was missing.

M. Lobry had left for Efesus. I had soon new proofs.

I had been with him to Aydin from 19th to 21st of February, and he was often interested in Efesus. At Aydin he told F. Philippe Pastel, Superior of the Mechitaristes, a man well known all over the country, as well as by himself. "I know about it", said the Father.-"I just have been attending to the question myself these last few days." "Some months ago", he continued, "a woman from Germany wrote to me and sent money, asking me to carry out research about the house described by C. Emmerich."

" I looked for it and I found it". "Did you find it?"

"Yes, an old church, very old, served by Greek monks." "Where is it?" "Not so far from Efesus. One can get there through Aziziye".

We went off from Aziziye, to go to Scala-Nova.

There it was at the bottom of the mountains. The place is called Dermen-Deresi.

F.Philippe's sayings prompted us to persist resolutely in the way we had started.

Thus, illuminated by F.Philippe, and stimulated by the Visitor, we had nothing else to do but wait patiently for the summer holiday. Meanwhile, we kept reading in the refectory the work of F.Duley, Dominican, a 3-volume work about C.Emmerich's visions, looking towards future research in order to find out more about them and also nurturing the enthusiasm and courage in our hearts.

Chapter II

Research and Discovery

The summer holiday came just in time. As soon as it started, I made use of my free time to accompany Brother Verney, who had been sick, to Constantinople. I was sick myself.

We had been on board since the 10th or 11th of July. Before disembarking, I met M. Jung and reminded him of our decision to dig at Efesus. That decision appeared to have been forgotten, for M. Jung seemed less enthusiastic.

- Do you think there will be opportunities to do this research?
- Yes my friend, why not?"
- Do you want me to go to Efesus?
- Of course I do, they gave us money for that:
- Well, I'll go, but:" .. (here a knock on the corner of the table), "I'll go, I'll dig all the mountain to be sure about this girl's visions and prove that it is only foolishness."

I left for Constantinople. Some days later, after my departure, the good M. Vervault arrived from Santorin, an old pontifical zouave of Charette and ex-soldier of 1870 like M. Jung, who was not at all opposed to adventures. He asked at once to participate in the projected expedition.

Good for them both, they accepted.

We started making our preparations. At once, when all was ready, we left for Efesus. It was Monday, July 27th 1891, the feast of Sainte Anne in the Roman Calendar, our calendar.

The members of the caravan were four:

M.Jung   -   Lazarist, chief of the expedition.

M.Vervault - Lazarist also, from Santorin House, being on
              holiday at Smyrna.

Thomaso   -   servant of the College, to take care of the
              luggage.

M.Pelecas -   M.Jung's friend, a free employee of the
              railway, who knew Efesus very well, for he
              had been station master there and was able
              to help our Confraternity's brothers to get the
              necessary information.

At Efesus a fifth companion joined us, in the person of good
Mustapha, black in skin, moslem in religion, hunter by
necessity. We trusted him, he knew his mountain well enough
to guide us, to show us the ways and he had his gun to keep
away evilly-disposed people and thieves, no rarity in these
parts. The group was composed as follows, in terms of religion:

-   3 Catholics, of whom two were priests
-   2 Greeks
-   1 Moslem

in terms of nationality:

-   2 Frenchmen (the two priests)
-   1 Greek (Mr.Pelecas)
-   1 Persian (Thomaso)
-   1 Turk (Mustapha)

All the evening was spent in visiting the diverse ruins of Efesus
and acquiring information.

M.Jung, - I don't know how- had imagined that he would ask
and be informed, that he would walk -according to the
directions given- and get just on with the task.

Mary's grave:

It was discovered with astonishment that nobody knew anything about it, nobody at the railway station, nobody even in the administration, nobody at the police station. It was terribly disappointing, a mishap.

It was decided, the same evening, that we should get to Aziziye by train the next day, and walk from Aziziye to Dermen-Deresi, and continue on foot to Scala-Nova. At Scala-Nova we would take some sort of vehicle to Ayassoulouk and sleep there at a small inn.

The plan was good, very good. On the one hand if we got through the mountains it would be possible to encircle, to limit the area of our research, on the other hand it gave us the possibility of visiting the place by getting through Dermen Deresi, and seeing, as F. Philippe Vasel had claimed to do, whether Dermen-Deresi was the place we wanted to discover.

After this decision had been taken we supped cheerfully, and having commended ourselves to the Lord, everyone took his dispositions for an excellent night, in order to meet the morning alert and in good condition, to face the next day's tiredness.

2nd day: Tuesday, July 28th 1891

The day after, Tuesday, at 4.30 in the morning, there was a general commotion. We got ready, we armed ourselves, five revolvers, one sword to five mountain rovers, plus a camera to immortalise curiosities on the road... Thus adorned we walked towards the railway station, Mustapha ahead, briskly, courageously, trusting deeply in Heaven.

At 6 o'clock we got on a goods-train to Aziziye. At 7 o'clock we got off at Aziziye, Having acquired some information we walked along a narrow path, deep, bushy, looking like a small gorge...

At 9.30 we encountered the first village, which was called Atchova.

I now give the word to one of the other members of the party, M. Benjamin Vervault, for whom I am copying the diary.

"No habitation in view, everything is silent and dull. We take a rest under the trees, waiting for Mustapha, who was sent to the village to look for a guide. We knew later that it was a Turkish village, except for one Greek family. So are the two others we shall pass through on our way."

Hearing the sound of our conversation, some women looked out of their windows.

Four or five children came later to play around the fountain. Here was Mustapha, who returned with a Turkish fellow with a red beard. Seeing our looks he got suspicious and moody. Meanwhile he accepted gracefully when promised a good bakshish to guide us as far as Dermen-Deresi. He took our bags and we followed him.

Three quarters of an hour later we came across two other Turkish villages[1] like the first, a small distance between them. The path went down. Finally we reached a narrow pass, and there was Dermen-Deresi. The monastery was very near. Eleven and a quarter exactly.

Before we entered, we stopped at the brook which runs over the path; we needed to wash our hands, to refresh our faces, to wet our palates. Some minutes later we were at the monastery.

All the Community gathered to honour us. The Community was composed of only two people: the Igoumen or Superior and his

---

[1] From Dermen-Dere to Aziziye there are three villages, whether left or right it depends on the path taken, Tchinar, Bourgas, Tcherkeskeuy.
Could it have been Tchinar where we stopped near the fountain to eat a piece of bread and drink a drop of water? That M. was the one Vervault had named Atchova.

assistant, a Brother. It was a perfect welcome; they invited us to come up to the first floor, where a Greek family still lived. That was good luck:.. They were M. Pelecas' friends...

They offered us coffee, mastica, refreshments, and the talking started while we were waiting for dinner.

Leaving our men to talk, we visited the monastery, which is 15 m. long, 7 m. high.

It looks a bit like Mount Athos.

The Monastery is a big building with a main gallery, and three rooms for pilgrims. It is built of stone, at the edge of a torrent. Above is the church, perched on a rock, also built of stone. It seems well kept, large enough. An orchard and a kitchen-garden are between the monastery and the church.

Slightly above, a brook supplies a mill standing above the monastery.

Dermen-Deresi is at the same time a place of pilgrimage and a sanatorium. Many people come from Scala-Nova. It is a charming place.

Texier, who visited it in 1850, describes it nicely:

"Half an hour from Scala-Nova one leaves the Sokia road, turning towards the North one crosses many hills covered with vines, most of them very well cultivated; then one enters a big valley irrigated by a small stream which runs into the sea in front of Samos."

"To the East there is a very picturesque path: vertical high rocks seem to protect the entry, while enormous plane and walnut trees form a maze of greenwood in the midst of which rise tall and elegant poplars. Nobody could find a site so wild and so fresh and delicious.... Going towards the pass there is a church, recently built. A water-mill makes you hear its monotonous sound..tic...tac..tic..tac.. A torrent runs down the mountain among the rocks."

"It is like being in a valley in Switzerland. There are in the vicinity ancient ruins. In the lowest part of the valley there are huge pieces of a building; three identical big stones, maybe rocks; it appears to stand on a salient basement 2 meters high. It appears to be the foundations of a grotto or marble fountain.

The waters probably ran through some undeground conduit no longer in existence.

The rest of the pile resembles the older Greek constructions.

Beside the church lies a granite column from an earlier age. This was found up on the mountain and rolled from its actual place by the calougers (orthodox monks). The church has its own history. According to an inscription above the door, it could have been built in 327. The most recent repairs, as a recent inscription placed also above the door tells us, date from 1812.

Here is the second inscription translated from Greek:

"....This church, buried underground, was discovered and excavated after a dream in 1812 by a pious man, to whom the Mother of God appeared at the same place."

The church was rebuilt from its foundations, under the inspection and direction of the Venerable Bishop who is the owner of the fountain, helped by pious subscribers under the order of Anthimious (?), famous among the monks of the monastery."

To all those who approach with piety the deliverance of soul and body is promised.- February 1814."

If one walks up the torrent, there to the left among the bushes is a road cut into the rock, dug partly by man's hand from where abundant water pours out. A channel at the side of the rock receives much of the waters and a huge aqueduct carries them as far as Efesus, over 50 km through the mountains, meandering 35-40 m above sea level.

Texier would willingly identify Dermen-Deresi with ancient Ortygia, so celebrated in Antiquity. Strabon says:

......"On the edge", cites Strabo," in the little wood above the sea is Ortygia; there is a magnificient wood, all kinds of trees, above all cypresses. It is a nice place, this wood, where Latona was delivered; the cavern of the Goddess, the Cenchrieus where she bathed after her deliverance, and the children's foster- mother, who was named Ortygia, and the olive tree in the shadow of which reposed Latona after childbirth."

"Above the wood is Mount Solmissus. The Curets settled on this mountain made much noise with their weapons to prevent the lamentation of the Goddess being heard by Junon, who spied jealously on the double childbirth."

"There are", goes on Strabo "Many temples in these places, some old, some recent. In the former there are wooden statues, in the second, new work-pieces. One can see Latona holding a sceptre and Ortygia, a child in each hand." Strabo L.XIV.

Nothing remains of all these edifices. Only near the monastery door are the remains of a cyma, in Greek style, perfectly sculpted, adorned with a lion's head which is half broken; but the topography, as Texier says, is exactly as described by the Greek geographer. The brook could be Cenchrieus, which pours into the sea in front of Samos. The mountain could be Salmissus. The distance between Dermen-deresi and Efesus in a straight line is 10 km. Whatever there could be of this identification there is nothing to interest us, so Dermen-Dere doesn't appear to have been seen by the visionary of Dulmen, so it is not the right place to look for.

It is dinner time, they are waiting for us. Let us enter.

The Igoumen presided over the table, there were ten of us around it: there are ten of us apart from the two monks, five of us plus three strangers. Women and children have dinner together. The appetite is good, so are the meals: rice soup, a dish of onions, a dish of excellent fish, cheese....a true feast for Lucullus.

After dinner M. Jung discoursed upon photography, and proposed to take some of all those present together. This was accepted with enthusiasm! As the light faded we all went in procession to the church.

"To show you I know something about it", said M. Vervault joyfully. I got out the tripod.

Thomaso, quicker than I, took the camera. Nine of us sat on the church steps.. The Igoumen was dressed as if for a ceremony, as was his assistant.

Taking the photograph took some time. Finally the sacramental:.. one two three, attention! It was done....We checked the plate... but there is nothing. The lens wasn't strong enough to take in all these people together. It was a disappointment, but we decided to try again the day after. This time we would be equipped better, we would succeed. Three o'clock, time to go. We thanked the Igoumen for his patriarchal hospitality without forgetting to donate some coins, which were received with visible satisfaction."Is it for the church or for me?"

"For your good hospitality. Sas efharisto poli poli"

We thanked and him went back to Scala Nova early.

We had sent the lugagge in advance to Scala Nova. A donkey loaded with bags had come to Dermen-Deresi and had gone back. The heat was intense and the sun added to our morning tiredness.

Could it have been wearness, or the intense heat or the friendly drinks taken for the monks' health? Pelecas, who had been zigzagging for some minutes, fell down.

We washed his forehead, his temples, his hands. He felt better. We were three quarters of an hour late.

At 5.30 we reached Scala-Nova, tired and exhausted.

We sat down in a cafe on the shore near the window to get some fresh air.

People were looking over at our men with curiosity, idly strolling up and down, gazing at them shamelessly. A young Turk 20 years old, his belly proudly loaded with enormous knives, came over to the window and looked in. We asked him to go away, but he did nothing. We warned him once, twice, three, four times, but he took no notice. Then began an avalanche of invectives in Turkish, Greek, French... But it was a waste of time. The fellow stood there like a copper statue. Pelecas, losing patience, pulled out his sword and rushed upon him to whack him, when the owner of the cafe came out. He made a sign to the young man who left as quietly as he had come.

Meanwhile all this fuss had made some noise; people gathered in front of the café "Fortunately they just came in time to tell us the carriage was there", said M. Vervault. We went off in a hurry, happy to escape from these curious people who were gazing at us as if we had come from the Moon.

We left Scala-Nova early but night was falling. The vehicle was old. I was scared it would break down on the way, the front part breaking off with Mustapha and the coachman, the rear remaining in place with all four of us in the night, in the middle of the road.

Leaving Scala-Nova, we climbed a long slope for nearly two and a half hours, We had to get down from the carriage to lighten the vehicle for the horses.

It was 10 o'clock when we arrived at Ayasoulouk, at the small inn of Elia near the fountain.

3rd day, Wednesday July 29th.

We were so tired on Tuesday that we got up late Wednesday morning. At 6 o'clock in the morning, benedicamus Domino.

Everybody was sleeping. We all felt the necessity to sleep, even M. Pelecas. However on M. Jung's sign we all stretched our limbs and got up. Our Legs were stiff, our feet ached but nobody complained. The hope of finding the House and the Grave filled us with such animation. We quickly finished our preparations, and set out to scour the countryside!......

M.Jung, whom anxiety had kept awake for part of the night, had the time to make a plan and consider it. Catherine Emmerich had said: approximately 3 or 6 and half leagues to Efesus, on the left side of the road coming from Jerusalem, on a mountain where you gain access through narrow paths, to the south of Efesus..

We could go on after these precise directions. We had to direct our steps towards the South, the top of a mountain being on the right, by the best paths if possible! We had to explore the place and have dinner later at Arvaia, where M.Jung, after consulting Mustapha, had brought provisions by post-mail. Now, let us walk, compass in hand....It was Saint Joseph's feast, also that of Sainte Marthe.

We started by a short cut between the small mosque and the fountain to get to the paved road; that means the road to Aziziye; Aidin, Jerusalem. For one hour everything seemed to be going right. The route ran straight across the plain, southward. We reached the mountains.

Meanwhile we stopped for one minute, hesitating: M. Jung seemed to see trees far up on the right, otherwise to the West.

" Mustapha, I see trees up there"
"There aren't any trees up there, Sir"
Mustapha supposed they were fruit trees....
"Let us go up there", said M. Jung again without saying any more.

Mustapha didn't know any other way to get up there except by a path, the old path to the mine. We got to this path, it was 9 o'clock and the sun was already burninig.

At the time when the mine was in use the path was quite visible, and frequented. Two years before, mining had stopped. Wind and rain had worn the path away, brambles and maquis had grown over it. The path was lost, all these brambles, maquis and torrents made walking difficult. The ascent becoming steeper, the burning sun, soon all one's body bathed in sweat, wet clothes sticking to one's limbs... In spite of everything we went on, wiping our faces, breathing, stretching... our legs could not walk any more; they refused to serve us, it was necessary to stop and take a rest, a breath.

From that point onwards the ascent was a calvary. Every hundred steps we stopped to wipe forehead, face and hands; we drank from a gourd to refresh and revive ourselves a little, then we got up heavily and climbed the steep path again.

It was later when the gourds had been emptied, there was nothing to drink, and our thirst was all-consuming, Pelecas, absolutely exhausted and parched with thirst lay down, declaring he couldn't go any further. He preferred to die instead...

"Tha pethano, tha pethano:" "I am dying," he cried, "I am dying"

I used force to make him stand up and start walking again. After many efforts we reached the road to Aziziye, not far from the mine, and the terraces over there.

On the first shelves of the terraces there were tobacco fields where women were working.

Pelecas ran towards them: "Nero! Nero!" (water)!

"We haven't any water," said the women, "But over there in the "Monastery there is a fountain," they added,pointing at a place 10 minutes further away.

M. Jung and the others stopped by the entrance to the terrace, looking around. He remembered what C.Emmerich had said about a high and well planted terrace towards the mountain top.

Meanwhile Pelecas came back, and rushed ahead, head bowed down, towards the fountain like a thirsty deer. He crossed fields and terraces, missed the underwood path which led to the Monastery, crossed the land above it without a word, went up the hill to the left of the hollow, between the castle and the house. The men, supposing that he knew the way, came after him. They walked as fast as they could through the brambles from crest to crest, finally up the last one where a peak rises over the hollow. The first screamed when he saw this view: "We are lost!"

We were trying to find our way, when all of a sudden further down the mountain on the other side of the hollow, on a plateau, we perceived plane trees and a poplar which rose up proudly towards the sky. "There must be water over there. Let us go.."

Everyone slid, rolled over, ran as fast as he could down the slope, crossed the torrent and the hollow, and climbed up again by short-cuts towards the plane trees.

It was noon or almost when we reached the plane trees. A fountain! ...We hurried towards it... Soon a head appeared shyly at the door of an old hut, gazing at us suspiciously.... Who were these people? Could they be inspectors from the police or administration?

The head went in and the man came out and approached our men... He was Yorghi the Moraite, Andreas' partner whom we would soon meet.

"What is this hut hidden under the planes?

It could have been a sanctuary, or ruins... But yes, it was an old sanctuary. Meanwhile Yorghi was talking to Mustapha and Pelecas while M. Jung examined the old sanctuary curiously.

Suddenly he remembered something: those fields and that terrace they had just crossed ....this ancient ruin...these rocks. that mountain behind...the sea in front, Samos and its innumerable peaks...what did it all mean? Could it be that without knowing it, they had found just the House they were looking for?

Good heavens!..Quickly, hurry!.. We must be sure!

The visionary says that from the top of the mountain where the house stands one can see Efesus from one side, and the sea from the other, the sea being nearer than Efesus.

"Can we see Efesus and the sea from the top of the mountain"?
"Yes sir, do you wish to see for yourself?"
"With all my heart! Is it far?"
"No, only five minutes. Come."

The man quickly went straight up the mountain. M. Jung followed him, Mr.Vervault and Thomaso, too, wanted to look.

Meanwhile Pelecas, exhausted, lay down on a mat to take a rest before dinner. Mustapha had gone for provisions bought in the morning at the cafe at Arvaia. Two coldjis (street-porter) had been there by chance. Our man took one of the horses to go and get back quickly.

M. Jung got to the top of Bulbul-Dagh. He looked. Yes it was the place.

To the North - east was Ayasoulouk, the plain of Efesus, the ruins lying there of the city of Prion like a horse-shoe.

To the West and South - West, the sea spread out, Samos was in view with its numerous peaks, looking like islands spread out in the middle of the waves.

It would be difficult to express the feelings that filled the soul of our explorer.

He was so moved by what he saw. With no doubt at all about the Grave he knew it was somewhere there, a few steps further.

Full of trust after this feeling of certainty, he called his men:

"Are there any graves?"
"Many, sir"
"I wish to see some of them."
"Nothing easier. Come with me."

He went down Bulbul-Dagh towards the terrace. On the way down he showed us some old Greek graves, very old. In every grave M. Jung hoped to find the One he was searching for, but in vain. None of the graves fits C. Emmerich's description.

We were on the terrace, there was nothing to do but turn back to the house by the known way. It was the way Pelecas could not find. M. Jung was disappointed about the grave, but happy about all he had observed by himself.

Meanwhile, while we were climbing the mountain and visiting the graves, the women had come down from the terrace to a little plateau below the sanctuary. Bowed over, they worked on the tobacco.

Andreas had come, also. He renewed his acquaintance with Pelecas, who had worked with him on the railways. Then Pelecas told him about the expedition, just a few words, nothing else.

"They are people looking for stones:"

"Like those foolish English", says Andreas with a good smile.

"However, I have here an excellent leg of wild boar, it is just the moment to serve it."

He hurried to prepare the leg of wild boar with a dish of potatoes.

As Mustapha came back with provisions and when the excursionists came back, they found two dinners instead of one.

It was late, almost two o'clock, everbody was hungry, very hungry. They hurriedly sat down at the table, well disposed to honour the meal. When I say "table" it is a way of saying "Everybody sat down on the floor, eating with their fingers from the same dish." Andreas, Mustapha, Pelecas and the other two started first.

Our appetites satisfied, we chatted a little. M. Jung explored the chapel again, after which he lay down like the others on the mattresses or "paplomas" to take a rest before the return to Ayasoulouk.

Neither that day nor the next did any question about the name given to the ancient chapel come out. But they spoke about the graves. Yorghi the Moraite believed they were looking for Mary-Magdelene's grave:

"Are you looking for Mary-Magdelene's grave?", he asked M. Jung, without explaining.

Jung answered his question with another question:

-"Have they also said something about the Holy Virgin's grave being in the neighbourhood?" He spoke casually.

-"The Holy Virgin's grave? No, sir. There is the grave of Mary-Magdalene!" M. Jung was astonished by this statement; he was amazed how a tradition could be falsified in people's mouths, and how they had referred to Mary-Magdalene just as "Mary."

Let us say, that Yorghi's words did not prove anything against Kirkindje's tradition; he was a Greek from Morea, a stranger to the region. He had spoken according to the beliefs of his country.

"Well", said Mr. Jung, without any comment on Moraiti's reflexion.

"Help us to find Mary-Magdalene's grave. If you find it, I promise you five liras bahchich".

Departure at 5.30

In spite of our plan to walk through Ayasoulouk or Arvaia as we had decided formerly, we followed a new route proposed by Andreas. The path led towards Lysimaque's Wall, not far from the Gymnasium. Andreas wished to serve as our guide, and he also offered his donkey for the luggage. An incident on the way back amused us. Near the ruins there was a wolf standing on a rock, gazing avidly at the goats. M. Jung fired a shot at him, but the distance being long, Mr. Wolf was not disturbed at all......It was the only shot fired during the whole expedition.

"My watch says it's 8.15", said M. Vervault when we came back home, a little tired but satisfied with our day because we could say: we looked for it and we found it.

Glory be to the Lord, Glory also to Mary, our Lord's Holy Mother!

4th day, Thursday July 30, 1891

36

Thursday belonged indirectly to Panaghia's history. M. Vervault left the expedition. Accompanied by M. Heroguer, who had come from Samos, he returned to Smyrna towards 4.30 in order to take the Messageries next day and be at Santorin the following Tuesday, where he expected to start his annual retreat.

M. Jung and his men set off again by train for Aziziye, and from there they returned to Dermen-Deresi, but he left the road at Atchova, the last village, and took another road on the right through Tcherkeskeuy. He had a promise to fulfil: he also to pick up the camera he had left there the day before.

Once they were back at the Monastery (at the same hour as the first time), our men were received as old friends. We talked, we had dinner, later we talked again. Afterwards we read the inscription above the church door: we commented on it, and we remarked Mr. Texier's error, who translated; Tols Papuel par fils de Brieis, the right meaning is: water sprung out, or for them pours...etc.

Finally we took photographs. These included views and also the priest with his church, the Monastery with the mountain behind it and the surrounding sites. At three o'clock it was time to go back to Scala-Nova, where we had decided to sleep.

Thursday wasn't lost in Panaghia's case. On the way back to Dermen-Deresi, M. Jung explored the right side of the mountain to be sure that Efesus and the sea were not seen from some peak, or from the top of Ala-Dagh (Solmissos) or from the mine. Thus, the sea could be further from there than from Efesus. It was an important point to clarify and this has been done.

It would also be interesting to know the ideas of the Dermen-deresi monks about this question. Today, our studies completed, we could guess the answer, but at the beginning it was not like that.

M. Jung had a talk with the Higoumenos: "Where do you think the Holy Virgin died?"

"In Jerusalem"

"Is that certain?"

"I merely repeat what has been said. You are a learned person, you know better than I do."

5th day, Friday, July 31 1891

The plan was to set out early from Scala-Nova, to stay at the cafe of Arvaia and from there to climb up to the Monastery.

We looked for a carriage: it would cost 5-6 medjidies. It was crowded, people had come from Smyrna because of the pilgrimage to St. Elie. We decided to go on foot. We took our weapons and luggage and went on.

It was ten o'clock, when after three hours' walking we reached Arvaia. Everybody felt the need to rest their poor legs: At the cafe there was among the customers a young Turk- whom we'll find later- Ibrahim, the famous nephew of Arvaia's old Bey. He had been nice to the men, he had them served at once. He did even better. He offered to guide them. As they refused politely, he offered his donkey to bring their luggage. M. Jung, wishing to thank such a nice man, wanted to offer him something. What? A drink?.. the Turk didn't refuse, but as a good Moslem, he declined to drink this liquor. Two long hours were spent talking and relaxing... it was so hot outside, why hurry? We dined at the cafe, taking our time... but ennui came soon, so we got up.

Even though not so steep as the Efesus side, the path is pure agony. It is an unseen path; always climbing, sometime we jump from rock to rock. After yesterday's tiredness, the day before and the morning, it would be hard even for the most strong and valiant. This time it was M. Jung's turn to faint.

Arriving at the rock, just before the end of the journey, ten minutes from the chapel, he stopped. Pelecas and the Negro and the luggage were ahead.

"Leave me," he said to Thomaso, who remained behind with him. "I can't go on any more".

"We are near, sir, let us go on, take courage!"

"No, no, I can't go on any more!..."

He sat down sweating, almost fainting. After a quarter of an hours' rest and a cup of water brought by Thomaso from the fountain, revived, he could joyously continue the remaining few hundred metres to the camp near the chapel.

It was 1 or 2 o'clock when they arrived. They took a rest. M. Jung could later occupy himself with what he had come for.

The whole evening was spent asking questions and looking around. It was then that M. Jung learnt from Andreas the name of the old chapel:

PANAGHIA-CAPOULI THE DOOR OF THE HOLIEST

This simple name shed new light on the discovery, and confirmed the authenticity of the ancient edifice.

M. Jung knew also that a big stone, a cross in relief cut on one piece of stone had been found on the way to Arvaia. Couldn't this stone be the last station of the Holy Cross, the only one with this sign?

He wished to look at this stone, which had been laid in the chapel. He saw it, and Andreas gave it to him on condition that he did not speak to anybody about it and he took it to Smyrna. At present it is with other stones in the Museum of Natural History. (see note)

The important thing was to establish the exactitude of C. Emmerich's descriptions and all that was known; and M. Jung, book in hand began to compare the whole and the details.

Many points were incontestable, but how many he missed! Some were in contradiction with the Visionary's sayings. Meanwhile, in general, there were many similarities.

After having observed the chapel at length, M. Jung wished also to look round the site. He discovered near to Kara-tchalti rocks with inscriptions in Hebrew. This coincided with the visionary's sayings. So a Hebrew colony had settled in the area. One more proof, or a better one, with more certainty.

To end the day joyfully we sat down for photographs. Andreas, Thomaso and Mustapha had the honour of the first photograph. In spite of the approaching night we were quiet; it had been decided to sleep on the mountain, to go down to Ayasoulouk the following day and catch the train to Smyrna.

Everybody settled under the plane trees and did their best to have a good night's sleep. One had a sleepless night, though, it was Thomaso!

"Up this mountain so frequented by outlaws, among unknown people, what could happen?"

"Will they not take advantage while we are sleeping to rush upon us, to rob us, to cut our throats? In order not to be robbed or have our throats cut, our good Thomaso stayed awake all night long, gun in hand, ready to shoot as soon as something moved.

...When daybreak opened morning's door with pink fingers Thomaso was still awake, eyes swollen, his head heavy, his face pallid and tired. We joked with him. He didn't appreciate it; he was full of his own self-sacrifice, congratulating himself on having saved us with his vigilance.

6th Day, Saturday, August 1, 1891; return

It was time to return to Smyrna. As we had a lot of time before our departure for Ayasoulouk, we searched the mountain all the morning. At two o'clock we left Panaghia for the railway-station. A train was coming from Aidin at 4.30.

Our men caught it. After it had stopped at every station they arrived in Smyrna at 7 or 8 in the evening.

M. Vedvault had just gone. My return from Constantinople being almost at the same time as Mr. Vervault's return from Panaghia, I had the time to meet him and tell him about the discovery of an ancient chapel in ruins, but so uncertain and without any precision was my description that I was asking myself what it could be.. "M. Jung found it!" he said. "He will explain it better than you, I haven't the time to know things well."

So, with some curiosity, he was waiting for M. Jung to tell him about it.

I can still see him in my mind, coming into my room in an usual mood, looking like a fox caught by a hen!..

-"Well?" I asked him
-"I think, Monsieur, we have found it"

A loud laugh welcomed this opening." Get along, with you, you comedian! Don't tell me fairy-stories!"
-"I assure you, we have found it"
-"What are you saying?"
- "The truth, sir"

It was hard to believe, but soon I was persuaded he was speaking seriously He told me how they had looked round, how they had found Panaghia without realising it and how they had found a ruin looking just like C. Emmerich's description.

The report made some impression on me. I wasn't convinced but I was excited, there was something to look for seriously.

-"All this is good", I said in conclusion.

-"I find it hard to believe, I want to see it before I say anything at all."

-"Do as you wish. I'll guide you to Panaghia myself."

-"Not this week, but next. Until then, keep quiet about it."

The Second Expedition

Wednesday, August 12th, the Feast of Santa Chiara. M. Jung and I slept at the French Hospital to be nearer the train, which was to leave a little after midnight.

Thursday, August 13 at 01.30 in the morning we took our places in a goods train leaving for Aidin. No seats, no benches, everyone settled in as well as he could, some standing up, some lying down, some on one side, others half-sitting on the corner of a piece of furniture. The journey was tiring and boring. The night was dark, it was impossible to see outside, the weather was chilly, almost cold. We stopped at every station, but how many? When the train started it was with the speed of an ox.

"Will we never get there?" Finally we arrived, at 7.30. M. Jung got us to Panaghia through Aziziye. Constantin Grollot, Sister Grancey's gardener, came with us with his gun, to protect us. After we had climbed a slope to the West of the railway about 30 m away from the tunnel we took a path which led us onward to the left of a small valley. After a long detour we reached the tunnel...We walked for a while after we had left it to go westward again. We reached the mountain, then we climbed a steep, rocky slope.

The sun was hot, but bearable; we had good, yes, strong legs and our feet, after a rest of six hours, were ready for walking again. The journey was joyful and brisk. It was ten o'clok when, without any stress or tiredness, we reached the big terrace next to the mine. Ten minutes later we were at Panaghia Capouli.

After M. Jung's repeated explanations I was looking for some similarities between Panaghia and C. Emmerich's descriptions. Similarities grosso grossmodo.

I confess I was quite astonished when, at first sight, details one after the other, details of great value appeared all of a sudden, just as C. Emmerich had indicated. Truth surpassed conviction. There was nothing to say.

- "Here are the rocks behind the house."

- "Here is the mountain above the rocks, from up there Efesus can be seen."

- "Here, we can see the sea in front of Samos, and the numerous hills of Samos."

- "The terrace we crossed right now when coming past the mine is high and well-planted."

"Strange, more than strange..."

"Let us look at the house."

"Two rooms, one at the front and one behind."

The room behind finished round a corner, with a window only on one side. In the room on the right there is an alcove: here is the room, here is the alcove.

"What is this big alcove we see in the Virgin's room? Where was the fire-place in the principal room? What happened to the room on the left?"

Finally, what does this third room, like an entrance hall, mean? C. Emmerich doesn't mention this room."

We then start, book in hand, to reconstruct things according to the visionary's words.

"Let us start from the fire-place. Where is it?"

Mr. Jung points to one of the corners. "Over there!" he says "No, C. Emmerich says it is in the centre. Listen, I'll read and you listen to what the book says."

"The house was divided into two parts by a hearth in the centre. Where is the centre?" M. Jung stands in the centre.... "I saw fire in the middle of the door...."

"Is it right? Perfect."

"Let us go on. Right and left in front of the hearth, two narrow doors lead into the other part of the house......"

"Well! ..the fire-place is here, everything fits the description well: the hearth in the centre divides the two parts, there is a place for a narrow door."

The Alcove

Reading over and over, again we recognise the Alcove.

We were less successful than in the room on the left. We walked round and round, searching for a sign. Of course it had existed, there was the arch which served as an entrance. We might have to be satisfied with this.

We were less lucky with the Vestibule: it was impossible to discover any trace.

Being fair players, we accepted the double fuss of it all. We couldn't claim to clarify everything at once, after all. Hadn't we seen enough to congratulate ourselves on our visit?

One thing was clear. Panaghia merited attention: there was really a mine to be exploited.

We returned to Ayasoulouk the same evening. Leaving Aziziye, the way we had in the morning, we took a shorter route, the one Andreas had taken with M. Jung, the path which goes round the hollows and ends near Lysemaque's wall, in the plain of Efesus.

As we set out on our way, M. Jung, his mind always full of the Grave, made us change our route, taking the one which led towards the mountain. He looked round for some place where he thought he would discover some likeness between this and the place described by C. Emmerich. That could be the place were the Virgin was buried.

It was a small plateau, covered with green grass, small flowers and small green trees; water coming from underground kept all this freshness alive.

We stood for a while to relive everything, to exchange opinions, to discuss things without reaching any concrete decision. After that we took to the road again, in order to get home before nightfall.

We got to Elias just as M. Jung had done on his first journey.

We had nothing in excess, neither for sleeping nor for meals; but in fact we had all the necessary things and everything was in order. What more could we want?

Friday, August 14, the Eve of the Assumption. Just before 4.30 we were back in Smyrna, very satisfied with our visit to Panaghia. All the richer for having more than one idea, and stronger in our resolution.

The Third Expedition

The visit to Panaghia had as a practical result, a definite decision: we would study Panaghia.

In consequence, the following Wednesday, August 19th, M. Jung went back to the mountain, taking all his time to study all the details at length, carefully and exactly.

With him were M. Borrel, Paul d'Andria, Heroguer, Pelecas and Constantin to take care of the provisions, and luggage, Thomaso still being ill after the consequences of the first expedition.

For the third expedition a whole week was spent in the area, looking round the countryside, the mountain, its sides and corners, measuring, drawing, taking pictures, noting down with exactitude every point, every little indicator that looked important.

Then the Castle was found, then the first Station of the Holy Cross was found, then the high place of Kara-Thalti, known as Calvary's Station, was found.

-"Isn't there a castle in the neighbourhood?"

-"No"

This astonished our men, but did not trouble their conviction.

They asked again. "Maybe one, two, three, four miles on?"

Finally the man spoke: "There may be. Are you talking about the Palaio Castro?"

"The old Castle?"

"Palaio Castro. Could be. Where is it?"

"A quarter of an hour away, between two terraces"

We got to the Palaio Castro. We had the satisfaction of proving one more time that what C. Emmerich had said was true: at 1200 m. from Panaghia we found the ruins of the old Castle.

Was it the way the Holy Cross? We knew nothing for the moment, but soon it would become apparent. Running in the direction marked by the Visionary, we found one by one the different places to look out for.

Here was a terrace made by human hand.

Around it was a stone wall.

There was a kind of pool marked by rocks placed there symmetrically further on, a level area with rocks like a cloister-wall.

Further on was a kind of enclosure bounded by stones arranged on end in a circle.

"What is this, Andrea?"

"I don't know, sir."

"Couldn't it be a place for coal?"

"Oh no! Surely not! If they had had coal, we would find coal ashes, but there's nothing like that."

"How long has this been here?"

"Oh; it is old, very old, I have seen it often and it existed before me."

"Are there other places like these in the area?"

"No, sir. Only here, not elsewhere....."

These strange sites, with equal distances between them, these irregular enclosures, different places but looking similar, these stones, stood on end... Did not all this make us remember the Stations of the Cross mentioned by C. Emmerich? Couldn't they be the remains of these primitive stations? Andrea's declarations strongly confirmed this hypothesis. Having thought it over, we concluded affirmatively, without imposing our opinions on anybody.

The station of Kara-thalti especially made an impression with its large enclosure with a clearly marked boundary, its high position; dominating all the line, it presented a particular physiognomy. It fitted in so well with the idea we had arrived at about Calvary, the whole context telling us that since the very beginning this name had been right.

These authentications, this research, had been done with faith and piety, also with many feelings, such as wishing to find, hoping to find, the joy when we had found something, the disappointment when we failed and we needed to research again.

Under the influence of these feelings and common impressions, a poet of the group, M. Heroguer, soon improvised a Cantique to fit the circumstances, on the Lourdes Cantique air.

It wasn't so rich as poetry, but only the emotion of the surroundings accompanied it:

1. What Gabriel said to you
in ancient times
is our Cantique now
Oh! Queen of Heaven.
Ave, Ave, Ave Maria

3. Show us, O Mother,
The Holy Cross Way
On this earth
You saw us pray.
Ave, Ave, Ave Maria

2. On this hill guide our steps
O, Divine Mother
Don't leave us ever
Never leave us
Ave, Ave, Ave Maria

4. One day pilgrims in life
through Mary
We dearly hope
The Divine place
Ave, Ave, Ave Maria

J. B. Heroguer, August 23, 1891

Oh! Mary! Remember our little singer on the mountain:

Protect him during his life! Protect him, most of all help him, bless him at the moment of his death.

We met morning and evening to sing this cantique to the Virgin.

In the morning we prayed to her to bless our Work, in the evening to thank her for the results obtained.

On Sunday August 23 we prayed and were present at the first mass.

It was the first mass at Panaghia. On the round massif of the sanctuary, Andrea, out of three old wooden shelves, had made a shaky table. On this altar M. Jung celebrated the mass, M. Heroguer was the choirboy. Andreas' wife and daughters were also present.

Some other Greeks were also present. They enjoyed this mass so much that they asked M. Jung to stay until August 27 to celebrate their own Feast of the Assumption. Due to the fact that our annual retirement started on 26 August, Wednesday evening, M. Jung could not accept the invitation. On 25 August he left the mountain with all his people and went back to Smyrna the same day.

Could it be said that everything was clarified? No! There remained still the vestibule, the octogon, to study better the room on the left, to label and completely authenticate the stations of the Holy Cross.

The Grave remained and still remains to be discovered.

This will take time, and labour and many subsequent visits. We will speak again about all these historic things as long as they are found and clarified .

Our period of retirement ended. M. Jung planned to send a report to M. Lobry, the Provincial Visitor, about everything concerning the discoveries at Panaghia.

Smyrna, September 30, 1891

Dear Sir and Brotherhood,

May Our Lord's Grace be with you forever:

Our expeditions to Efesus and surroundings have ended, our retirement, also. During these last days I have prepared photographs and plans of the results concerning our work.

Before starting my report, permit me to say that I believe in accomplishing a duty of conscience and filial piety, our August Sovereign Mother, permitting, as I write you these lines. God's things are done independently of humans. It is right that they, as his humble servants, are His instruments, and the instrument must be properly docile in the workman's hands.

I had left Smyrna with the thought of finding C. Emmerich at fault. I confess I had little trust because as you know, I am an indifferent admirer of visionaries.

I came back with the certainty that there is, right down to the smallest detail, perfect conformity between the datum of the Sister and the photograph described by her, mathematical exactitude between what she says about the House, the Calvary, the Stations of the Holy Cross Way and what we discovered.

I say certainty, not persuasion, because being defiant of myself, I took with me to the sites M. Vervault, Poulin, Heroguer, d'Andria, Paul and Borrel, Director of the French Post Office. We surveyed the site, as objective and severe as men who don't wish to be ridiculous must be.

After six days of research and land surveying, Borrel the expounder of us all, resumed as follows:

"Even if one million surveyors should come, all of them would say: "Only one who really saw could write and describe like this."

She has seen the Good Sister, the sites and things, all this defies contradiction, everyone can come and see as we did.

She has seen through spiritual eyes, then; causa finita est.

The only thing we can say is: "Here is Mary's House:"

Here is the Cross, here are the grooved stones, let us kneel down and pray.

Could it be that this girl was wrong and misled the others.?

Brentano was either presenting accounts of some old and one-day travellers, a gratuitous hypothesis, an improbable, an impossible hypothesis.

1. Gratuitous Hypothesis: Where are the proofs? The Sister and her secretary looked like honest people. The research proves their sayings exactly, confirming their honesty.

2. Improbable Hypothesis: For what reason should they deceive us? Why should they have invented a Virgin's House at Efesus, a Way of the Holy Cross, a sepulchre, at the risk of turning against her an established opinion which placed Mary's death and grave at Jerusalem?

3. Impossible Hypothesis: The Sister describes things as they were in the Apostles' Time; she also describes things we found underground, like Hebrew inscriptions, the olive tree grove, the Grave which will also be discovered without any doubt, as soon as we are able to dig freely and seriously.

She sees Cayster following Pausanias; but these particularities, even though seen by the traveller, don't interest the Holy Virgin, nor those around Her.

A fresh and clear fountain pours forth only ten steps from the House.

It is visible, this fountain, as there is not another nearby. The Sister who travels in spirit does not feel thirsty, she does not mention the fountain, while about the house she gives the smallest detail of construction and place distribution.

Her silence about the Efesus monuments is also astonishing! She sees underground what the traveller or the pilgrim do not see, she keeps silent about it is seen by all...

It seems to me that this thesis is serious, logical, and even a severe critic could approve it. After all, I am not in charge of forming public opinon over C. Emmerich' morality nor that of her secretary, Brentano. It is for everyone for study, to examine, to judge.

Their life, as we know, doesn't permit us to doubt it as dishonest.

As far as the Sister is concerned, God almighty gave an irrecusable witness to her virtue, her stigmata and other supernatural gifts, to be represented by the French Government and the German Protestant Government.

The Bishop of Münster himself examined her lengthily and minutely. Only then did he designate Clement Brentano to be the Visionary's confidant and personal Secretary.

What else remains for me to do, Mr. Visitor, unless to invite you to come and see for yourself, and you'll see and give to our research the support of your high authority.

I'll be happy and honoured to escort you to Panaghia Capouli, where you have been yet with Sister de Grancey, one of the promoters of the enterprise. Meanwhile, let me glance at the plans and photographs I will send to you with brotherly respect.....

Here M. Jung takes point by point the House and site, he establishes similarities between what he himself saw, and those described by C.Emmerich. As we have the opportunity to review at length the ecclesiastic official report, I resume.

He says of the road, which was described by C. Emmerich:

"This road has always existed. It runs alongside the railway from Efesus to Dinair, old Apame, passing through Tralles and Aidin. There is an old Roman way, half paved, used by the caravans."

He says about the terrace:

"The cultivated terraces marked on the plan are the only places in the Efesus mountains; many in the surroundings are suitable to be cultivated."

He says about the Colony:

"Old graves prove that Bülbül-Dagh has been a place of abode. As for houses, there is not any vestige left."

He mentions rocks behind the House and the mountain:

"12 m. South-West of the house, rocks rise up 520 m. above sea level. After these rocks is the mountain, from the top of which one can see Efesus to the North-East and the sea to the West, with Samos in view."

He says of the Castle:

"The castle overlooks the terrace. It is of similar concruction to the towers of the ramparts built at Efesus by Lysimaque. Thus it dates back to the 3 rd century B.C.

"As for the House, it will be included in whatever is written in the official report of inquiry."

The entrance can be explained thus:

"The entrance has been added more recently, probably by the Apostles themselves. According to the Visionary they transformed the Virgin's house in to a church."

He says about the Way of the Holy Cross.

"I have no pieces of conviction to send you-so I only declare what we found:

- One stone with a cross in relief.
- Three movable stones with inscriptions not deciphered.
- Three other inscriptions in Hebrew. These are more important than the others.

He adds:

The sites where these movable stones have been found, also the inscriptions; spaced between them, there are other landmarks which show the direction of the Way of the Holy Cross. There is no doubt about its existence.

He speaks about a cavern on the left of the valley after the little wood. Country people have no know ledge of it. It could be the Cavern of the Agony:

He continues:

"With the Sister, plan in hand, we started from behind the House, towards the little wood. We crossed the valley, eyes fixed on the cavern, we climbed the Kara-thalti to reach the Calvary, after stopping at the last inscriptions we looked around us....

If we had eyes sharp enough to penetrate, we would perceive the Holy Sepulture hidden under the ground, then we should fall on our knees to venerate, to pray:

Show us, O Mother,
The Holy Cross Way
Which in this land
Saw you so many times
Ave Maria

M. Jung ends his letter, he signs it first, the next person signing after him: M. Borrel, M. Heroguer, M. Paul d'Aridria.

Chapter III

Panaghia Capouli

1. Panaghia when discovered

Its Environment first, the House or Chapel later.

The place was uninhabited. There was only a path leading one way to Aziziye, the other to Arvaia. Only Andreas used to come to that place, for tobacco, with a partner or by himself, to cultivate or to reap. His cultivation consisted of two terraces bordering the castle, two or three bits of fields between the hollow and the houses; that was all. He paid for that 45 medjidies as rent every year, the rest of the land was uncultivated, abandoned. The mountain reached down as far as the path, towards the stream.

When one came from the Castle to the South, one saw firstly the plane trees. On the left down the path, under the shadow of the planes, a hole like a pool gathered the water used for irrigation. The fountain is still there, the pool also, but cemented, transformed. On the right, there is a second fountain on the path back by a small wall; on this small wall, a narrow, angular terrace going as far as the Virgin's room; opposite this terrace is a water-way dug by hand, which seemed to link the two fountains to the spring which flowed in the middle of the Holy Virgin's room.

The small fountain, small wall, small terrace and the trench all disappeared because of work done later to enlarge the level ground in front of the Chapel. One can still see it in old photographs.

To the North, Andreas had erected some light structure for his own accommodation.

Firstly a terrace sufficiently big.

This is the one that leads to the Chapel; two plane trees and one wild vine shadow it. On the terrace, in the North-East corner back in the rock there is an oven to cook bread. Further down the terrace near the path, a hut made of branches stands on four stocks, looking like a dovecote. This was where Andreas and his family slept during the summer. Further on at the place where our House stands there is a small hut with rough walls, thatched roof and two openings like doors. This hut serves to keep tools, provisions, crops, and in winter to lodge people and also animals.

This part has been worked on and repaired...

That was how it was in the past... The terrace is still there, but the oven, hut etc. are no more; cultivated terraces, fruit-trees, kitchen-gardens, new constructions have replaced all this. Now there are only photographs of the old days.

The Chapel; It was like today, surrounded by eight beautiful planes, bound together by a wild vine; in front of the plane trees, 5-6 m. from the path are slender poplars standing apart from the planes, their elegant peaks like arrows towards the sky.

The ancient chapel appears. Beautiful and venerable with an air of something discrete, it stands religious at the foot of the rocks.

At the foot of the mountain which shelters and overlooks it, the chapel stands under enormous trees that seem to protect it jealously with their shadow; every trunk seems like a bulwark; a slim poplar soars skywards, balancing gracefully in the air.

It looked like a guard who looks far into the distance to detect the approach of an enemy, like a mast to serve as rallying point, saying to the pilgrim:" Come, it is here!" But thunder struck it down some time in the last few years.

This is a pity; one liked to see it indicating the of the location House. It is missing from the landscape now.

Outside, the Chapel's walls were half-buried. On three sides, the level of the ground was halfway up the wall, that is, the East side and South side of the room said to be the Holy Virgin's.

Inside the building:- An ugly door opened into the Vestibule, the Vestibule as it is today. The wall on the left was half-destroyed in the middle; the rest of the place was as it is today. In the sanctuary, the two lateral gothic elements are surrounded by old, strong stonework, one part being ugly stone-work more recent than the other part. In the sanctuary, the stone block was intended to serve as an altar.

A big carved stone above the stone block was found on the ground in the same place where the altar is today. As C. Emmerich said, this was the stone upon which St. John celebrated the mass... Could this stone be the old stone of St. John? On the stone were the remains of small candles, like the ones the Greeks used to burn to honour the Virgin. There was an alcove to the left of the altar in the corner; inside the alcove was a packet of small candles plus two icons depicting. St. Michael, St. Demetrius or St. George killing the dragon. There was a roof but no floor. On the walls, two or three trees served as girders; on the girders, reeds served as joists, letting the light, the rain, the wind, the sun and air pass through. It served to dry tobacco....

On these reeds tobacco leaves had been hung to dry. There was nothing inside the sanctuary, out of respect for the place. The bare ground served as the floor. 20-25 cm. High, it was surrounded by a circular wall, this being before the inner door, so the door could open easily.

The Virgin's room: The Virgin's room was separated from the chapel by small arches. There one could enter only from outside through the sole opening near the big plane tree. This room was completely bare. No tiles, no floor, only the bare ground, an empty space of 15-10 cm. under the small arch, under also the threshold of the door, and the big alcove, and also the stone circle which ends there.

The big niche: in the middle of the floor was a hole approximately 0,60 m. deep, which served to store water to feed the fountains below; but for some unknown reason the water had stopped flowing; there was a little water only at the bottom of the hole. All the rest of the room was the same as today.

We promised each other to leave the Chapel as we had found it, in spite of the fact that some work needed to be done, without changing any part of it, keeping the original shape.

The main part of the house: - a new door had replaced the ugly old one; in the wall on the left, the two arches had been opened; a provisional wooden table served as an altar, but later a marble altar was put in. The ground had been excavated, revealing the old floor and pavement.

The Virgin's room: A sliding grille served to close the aperture near the plane tree to prevent dogs and other animals from coming in.

The hole has been lined with bricks, the ground levelled, a small altar has been put in the alcove, which was previously empty, to satisfy the devotion of pious pilgrims who wished to celebrate holy mass in the Virgin's room, also making it possible to celebrate two masses when there were two priests at the same time. To complete these restorations, some cement has been used here and there to prevent deterioration. Finally, a suspended roof has been erected over the entire roof to cover it and protect the building and shelter people during rainy weather; some sacrifices were necessary for this roof: some branches of the plane trees had to be cut off -for they extended into the chapel- the wild vine also had to go. Had it not been cut down, the roof would have collapsed.

After this work, the building remained in its original form, as it was when discovered.

2. Panaghia in the past

There are further memories concerning Panaghia dating back about sixty years; we collected them piously and seriously, noting them with the greatest exactitude. In these days the mountain was full of trees. There was an old Turk who made money by allowing people to cut and burn wood for 60 piastres every 6 months. Thieves had made of this place their general quarter!.. It was quite impossible for a stranger to get through these parts without being in danger of being arrested, robbed even killed. Only the country people were able to get through; a freedom they bought for themselves from the thieves by giving them bread, a sheep or other provisions.

At that time the chapel was a ruin, an accumulation of rubbish. Brambles and bushes grew everywhere. In spite of this ruin, this desolation, the old chapel was not abandoned. The people of Kirkindji used to go there and pray, celebrate the holy mass.

Since time immemorial they had come on a pilgrimage to this place, every year, particularly in mid-August in memory of the Holy Virgin's death.

"On the eve of the pilgrimage," says a witness, "Male volunteers used to come and clean up all these brambles around the chapel. On the day of the feast men, women, young girls, young men and children arrived with the priest. They set up a provisional altar on the ruins. After the mass they dismantled the altar, and after a rest they went back to Kirkindje."

All these details are from Andreas of Kirkindji, one of the elder witnesses of Panaghia.

On 9th of May 1894, the Wednesday before Pentecost, Andreas came from Panaghia to Smyrna; we profited from his presence to ask him all he knew about Panaghia.

Here is the result of this interesting but simple inquiry, the questions and answers:

Question: Since when have you known about Panaghia?

Answer: Since the age of five, from my father; today I am 50 years old, so I have known for 45 years.

Q. How long have you been going to Panaghia?

A. For 30 years.

Q. What was Panaghia like before your time?

A. My father came sometimes but he didn't remain more than two years. Before him it was "eremos" (desert)."

Q. In what condition did you find Panaghia?

A. The terrace in front of the chapel didn't exist; I built it, also the wall to support the terrace. A long time before, brambles and bushes blocked the entrance, every time we wished to come to celebrate the mass, we had to come in advance to clear the way. I cut back the brambles, cleared the entrance and made the terrace.

2. The room on the right, known as the Virgin's Room, was quite the same as today; the walls were in the same condition, the floor had a hole in it, just as it has now; the fountain in the middle of the room was as one can see it now. In the entrance an old, rough door opened into the room. I didn't touch it, I only closed the arch which separates the chapel from the room. Before this closure, one could get to the room from two sides: from outside through the outer door and inside through the arch.

3. The front face of the Vestibule is as it was, just the same; I only put some stones there to strengthen it.

4. Inside the Chapel, the side walls of the square room had collapsed, mostly in the middle of the chapel, approximately as far as the paintings; I built them up again until they were the same level as the other, and also made the two existing windows.

5. The wall of the last room had fallen down, though not completely, only in the middle where the alcove and the altar are now. The two massive sides at the back were not in ruins. From the breach in the lowest part of the wall the ground had fallen away, forming a slope. It was easy to get in and out or up and down through there and even a walnut tree had sprouted there. I pulled it up and closed the breach at the bottom; I made the window and the niche you can see now, also the altar under the alcove.

Q. Why did you make this niche?

A. Because it is like this in our churches.

Q. Did you find anything from earlier times while cleaning up?

A. No, I cleared everything away as far as the foundations; I just dug a little.

Q. What did you find?

A. Two skeletons, and a big stone; that is now the altar and in front of it I found the two skeletons.

Q. What do you think about the two small niches?

A. They are old; I suppose they put the holy communion there. They are tabernacles.

Q. In what condition did you find the room on the left?

A. The same as now, only the small arch was open. The vault was open but I closed it. The rubbish was piled up high, thus it was quite hard to get in or out through there.

Q. In what condition was the chapel's interior?

A. Full of rubbish. I cleared it away; for less work I made the small wall at the entrance of the chapel where the door opens. I made this wall to keep back the rubbish that I didn't want to have to carry away.

Q. What is your opinion about the two columns in the two angles of the inside door?

A. They are old. I found them like this.

Q. Thus, you made the terrace of the entrance,

- you built up the side walls of the square area,

- you made the two windows, right and left,

- you closed the two big arches,

- you repaired the wall at the bottom,

- you made the big alcove in the middle with the window above.

- finally, did you also make the altar under the niche?

A. Yes, I did.

Q. What kind was the rubbish in the chapel?

A. Stones, bricks, lime, earth.

Q. Did you celebrate mass at Panaghia?

A. Yes. I asked for that to be done many times.

Q. Who else asked for its celebration?

A. Only the people of Kirkindje; Nobody else

Q. Did you celebrate mass often?

A. Two or three times a year.

Q. You told us the church was full of rubbish!....

A. Yes. We prepared a temporary altar on top of the rubbish. Once the mass had been celebrated we left the altar there.

Q. Did you ever see strangers at Panaghia?

At this question Andreas smiled and made a gesture, full of significance: "Never," he said.

Q. But why?

A. Because no stranger would dare to come hereabouts because of the risk of being captured by the robbers who have settled in the mountains.

Q. But what about you? How could you remain there? And what about the people of Kirkindji?

A. I am different! I am a poor man; what could they take from me, or do to me? Of course, I give them tobacco, coffee...

In spite of all that, I have been arrested twice.... As for the people of Kirkindji, they are countrymen; the robbers don't touch the village men.. But strangers are different!

Q. Since when has the countryside been safe?

A. For seven years only, since they executed the last chief, Osman, at Konak.

Q. What do you think about the spring-water in the room?

A. It is an ayasma, sacred water.

Q. Did you find around the fountain any marble, bricks, stones or whatever?

A. No! No, The spring-water was the same as now.

When the people of Kirkindji came to Panaghia, did they celebrate the mass in the spring-water room or in the chapel?

A. In the chapel, not in the room.

Q. When they went up, did they go for the water or for the chapel?

A. Andreas shook his head: "For the church! Not for the water."

Q. According to you, what purpose does the big niche in the spring-water room serve?

A. I suppose they used to celebrate mass, also.

Q. Why do you think that?

A. Because in our churches they celebrate mass in places like this.

Q. Are there places like this to celebrate mass in your churches?

A. No, only one.

Q. In your churches is there a room on the right and left of the place where mass is celebrated?

A. No.

Q. Let us come to the fountain. When you came the first time, did the fountain run out like it does today?

A. It was like it is today, in the middle of the room. I only cleaned up; but down on the terrace it ran out in many directions.

Q. Did you ever seen water flowing out through the five holes seen in the wall?

A. No, never! Maybe it happened years ago, when we had heavy rain. Afterwards, two springs appeared, one in the chapel precisely where the walnut tree was; I uprooted it. The other spring was outside near the oven; water was flowing out through the chapel.

Q. How long did these springs flow ?

A. Almost two months; then they stopped, they disappeared underground.

Q. What is this wall between the path and the room with the spring ?

A. It is an old wall.

Q. Were there paintings in the church?

A. No, I didn't see any paintings.

Q. What is the real name of the chapel?

A. Panaghia Capouli. They say the Church of Panaghia Capouli, the fields of Panaghia Capouli, the woods of Panaghia Capouli, the mountains of Panaghia Capouli.

Q. Panaghia Capouli or Panaghia Capelli?

A. Isn't it the same ?

Q. What is the meaning?

A. The name's meaning is: 'Door of the Holiest', or 'Virgin's Door'.

Q. What do you think about those terraces on the mountains along the way ?

A. They are old; they have always been there.

Q. Are there similar terraces elsewhere on the mountain ?

A. I know only these ones.

Q. Couldn't they be old coal yards?

A. No! Firstly the place is not suitable. There would be traces of ash and coal, the grass wouldn't grow there...

Q. What do you think they could be ?

A. I don't know. (It is what they call: "The Holy Cross Way Stations.)

Q. Was there a forest at Panaghia before?

A. Yes; a big forest with big trees. They were destroyed thirty years ago.

Q. How did that happen?

A. The Turk gave to whoever wanted, for sixty piastres, permission to cut down trees for fuel; you could take as much you wanted for six months. Thus all the forest was destroyed. Before that, all the mountain was covered with trees.

Q. How did they get to Panaghia?

A. The same way you got here. That was before the new road was made.

Andreas spoke like that; freely, comfortably, on the day above indicated in the presence of M. Poulin, M. Jung, and

Constantin Grollot, who was there as interpreter and third witness.

This was repeated also to M. Timoni who called on us, came by chance some minutes later to question Andreas; thus, all that has been reported has been certified.

Andreas' story shows well enough what Panaghia has been like for the past fifty or sixty years; but what was it like between Mary's death and our time? What happened in the eighteen centuries which preceeded us?

Who will tell us?

Some things seem to be true; others are uncertain, even obscure: they will be probably remain like this until the end of the World.

I. The Locality

1. It seems the locality has been inhabited since very old times; This is testified by the remains of old walls, old houses which still exist and are discovered after every excavation.

Who were the habitants? Greek country folk? Jewish refugees? Did Christians come later, wishing to live where Mary had lived and died? Maybe all this could be discovered, for there are graves of different shapes with lacrymotories found inside them; there are inscriptions or some Hebrew letters engraved on some rocks. Elsewhere, Christian signs can be found in the ruins.

2. It seems that there was a particular Establishment in the centre of Panaghia, exactly where our House is.

This Establishment existed centuries ago, as it appears from some signs, especially some medallions found which date from the 4th, 5th and 6th centuries. This Establishment must have been important, judging by its remains. There was once a pool, arches and colonnades, vaults, stairs, mosaics, platforms like terraces, many massive walls, finally many water-pipes running from many sides.

This Establishment had been there since the 5th century, was Christian, almost certainly religious and ecclesiastical; this is proved by the mould of terra-cotta found among the ruins, also pieces of broken glass. Could it be the Episcopate which C. Emmerich speaks about? Was it a Monastery, as the common name of "monastiri" given by the people would lead us to believe?... We will never know...

When was all this destroyed? This probably took place centuries and centuries ago, as it seems from the strata of ground accumulated in the ruins, also by the complete lack of more recent materials. That is all that can be said.

How did this building become a ruin, also why was it completely abandoned? Judging by the position of the columns lying on the ground in a North-South position among other remains in the middle, it seems that an earthquake from North to South took place. The scared inhabitants went away and never came back again. The desert remained the only master. The passage of time covered these ruins so well; nothing remained except a name: "to monastiri", the monastery.

II. The House or the Chapel

It is immediately obvious that the House or Chapel have been restored many times, in different periods, maybe rebuilt, but always in the same place on the same foundations.

According to C. Emmerich, the House was transformed into a Church by the Apostles after Mary's death. Maybe then the fireplace was pulled down; also the stone floor was covered with earth, in the same place, where with surprise and admiration all would be found in the same place with everything in order, 1800 years later.

A total or partial reconstruction followed, it seems, this first transformation; it can be seen by the difference between the structural disposition of the walls and the primitive structural disposition of the foundations.

In which century was total or partial reconstruction done? It could have been in the 3rd, 4th, 5th or 6th, when the Emperor Justinian in 550 built the church of St. John not far from the temple of Diana, on the hill of the Castle, the huge, rich basilica which gave its name to Ayasoulouk, Aghios Theologos, the St. Theologian.

Could it be later? Could it not be an even earlier period? Maybe the first century? Couldn't this reconstruction have coincided with the transformation of the House to a Church by the Apostles?

M. Carre, an architect of the Ministry for Foreign Affairs, also an archaologist have scrupulously examined the Panaghia monument, the whole and the details. His statements are surprising, for according to him:

"The thickness of the angular walls indicates a public building that was intended to remain eternal". He continues: "The big arches at the sides are old, very old, could be first century A.D". Also according to him:

"The big niche of the Virgin is a kind of Hebrew architecture."

Whatever happened, it was then that the Chapel acquired its first and definitive shape; it was then that the small outside door which gives access to the Virgin's Room was opened. At that time or a little later the vestibule was added to the primitive masonry in the same era, confirm the experts, but added later. The proof is undeniable, at the beginning there was just an ordinary house; it had three rooms, one in front for guests. It was later that the house was transformed into a chapel.

One could assume a third restoration, in the Byzantine period, from the ornamentation of the outside walls. If one follows the North wall of the Chapel, the Byzantine ornamentation starts from one side at the end of the wall, and continues without any interruption. Subsequently the room on the left disappeared; or maybe during the ornamentation work it was demolished.

It is easy to suppose that the Chapel shared the same destiny as the Central Building, and was severely shaken by the same earthquake, but its more solid, stronger masonry resisted the tremors; only the roof and the vaults collapsed; the mass of the building resisted and stood up; but the Church was in ruins and full of rubbish.

For centuries and centuries no pious hand cleared the old chapel or to tried to rebuild it from the ruins; it remained until our time in the same sad condition. It seems, however, that, in spite of the ruin and desolation, it has never been completely abandoned. The Efesians kept going to pray and honour Mary, as is seen with the people of Kirkindji, the natural heirs of their traditions and practices. As before, the people of Kirkindji have gone every year to pray at Panaghia, to celebrate masses, and have made pilgrimages, particularly on Assumption Day.

It pleased the Lord to leave Panaghia to French Catholic hands; could the same Divine Goodness take over the helm again at Panaghia and, with ardent piety, restore the Chapel to its former splendour...

Chapter IV

The Purchase of Panaghia

It was on 29th July, 1891 that Panaghia was discovered; the following 15th August a first review was decided on, to be continued from 19th to 25th of the same month. A third, long inquiry was held and it was established without doubt that "they had found what they were looking for, there was no need to look elsewhere."

Soon people started saying, "How good it would be if we had this!." Later they said: "We must have that!." Then they said: "We must have this!." The idea made its way little by little into their spirits. So far so good; the decision had been taken to acquire, but what about the possibility!..

Could we buy it? We couldn't think about it with this enormous debt of 300-400 thousand francs.. with a return of zero! Otherwise, Paris would never permit a similar acquisition; to whom could we turn? We didn't wait for long!...

The Lord, who sees and organises things, had taken care to put before us a soul in love with beauty and goodness, who was ready to give herself to everything good. A great soul, devoted, ardent, pious and generous; the noble Sister Marie de Mandat Grancey. She was, God has chosen her to be the terrestrial Providence, like Panaghia's Mother! For twelve years she has been charged of this valiant religious enterprise; she has never failed.

Oh! How happy I am to give her all the respect she merits! Also, could these writings make known to posterity, long after us, to whom France, the Catholic church are in debt for Panaghia! The Lord gave me this opportunity to say loudly what I had in my heart for a long time, to acquit what I deemed to be a serious debt. It is done. Praise be to God!..

For years Sister Grancey had been thinking about the Virgin's Grave, looking forward to its discovery. As soon as she had been told about the opportunity of buying Panaghia, her heart was full of joy.. "Just the time to find the necessary funds," she answered: "Do let's buy it."

We felt very embarrassed.

We didn't know who the owner or the seller was, so we couldn't ask in order to find out. It was also important to be discreet, not to make any noise in order to prevent jealousy and disputes; to be careful of the intrigues of such and such who could have an interest in its acquisition, perhaps to stop us buying it, or to substitute themselves for us. It has, however, been decided between M. Jung, M. Binson and me to go to Efesus; on the way we would prepare our plan, commending ourselves to the Lord's Grace; we would try to discover what we could do for the best. The day of the journey: Wednesday, January 27th 1892.

The Wednesday came, we set off for Efesus. As soon as we had settled in the train and started to speak about our project, the door opened and a gentleman with a fez on his head, a kindly face, quite young, came into our compartment. A Greek, perhaps? Oh! bad luck! We could not speak about our business! A wasted journey......

Also, we couldn't say to this man: "Get out, Sir! You are disturbing us, you are hindering us from speaking". We exchanged glances, we gave up in despair.

M. Binson desired to learn who he was.. After some minutes of silence he offered him a cigarette. He accepted politely. "Are you going far, sir?" asked M. Binson. "As far as Scala-Nova, sir". Scala-Nova! as far as us... and further!. Goodbye, plans.. Goodbye, projects...

"Scala-Nova? repeated M. Binson. "Are you from this country?". "Oh no! but I have worked here for a while for M. Missir"

"Who is Mr. Missir?"

"Missir from Samos."

"Oh! We know him very well. He's from Smyrna, too!"

After having a chat about acquaintances and business, the stranger started on Scala-Nova's gossip. "Oh! "he said," A curious affair is going on now at Scala-Nova. Half of Efesus and its territories are owned by a rich old Turk who lives at Arvaia, named the Bey of Arvaia; the other half is owned by his nephew, a Turk and Moslem like his uncle. The uncle is an old thief, an old rascal; the nephew is no less rascally than the uncle, but with this difference; the uncle is as stingy as the nephew is prodigal. The young fellow spends and wastes; so he hasn't got a penny in his pocket and owes money to everyone. To live and pay his debts he borrowed 2000 gold liras from his uncle. The old man lent his nephew 2000 liras, but as he distrusts him, he took out a mortgage on the young man's land. Actually the old man needs money and claims his 2000 liras; the young man hasn't got the money, so there is a lawsuit. The old man would like to force the young man to hand over his part of the land to cover the 2000 liras, plus some interest...They are locked in dispute, they threaten each other, no one knows how all this will end:... But here we are at Ayasoulouk.. Good morning, sirs!.. Good morning, sir and have a good journey!"

Oh, God in Heaven! We had cursed this man's presence, but he, without any doubt, had revealed to us what was the most important thing for us to know. The land was divided between the uncle and the nephew. Both of them needed money. They were involved in a lawsuit for the land... Did we need more information? There was nothing to be asked. We knew everything, without asking, without revealing our identities, our projects; and blessed be the stranger, met by fortunate opportunity.

Providence! Providence!

Under these conditions we had no other choice than to go directly to the Bey; so we did. We caught the public coach, which after a one-hour journey set us down before the café at Arvaia.

We had been travelling from Smyrna since the morning. The sky was clouding over little by little. It started raining while we were on our way to Arvaia. We stopped and went into a café.

Seated, or rather, having climbed up on to a chump of wood, we were waiting for some blow. It came so suddenly, it was extraordinary for the season. I was asking myself if it wasn't devil's stroke to stop us proceeding... For half an hour the tempest caused great disorder, thunder, lightning, rain all wrestling violently; one wouldn't put out a dog in it. Ten minutes later the road become a torrent; a stream covered it, rolling down, dragging along all kinds of rubbish. The sky was melting in water; rain came down in a flood. I can still hear the crash of the water on the ground. I can still see this overflowing stream closing our every route...

If it was the devil's stroke, the devil had decided to get his own back!!

In spite of losing courage, the storm stimulated both us and our trust in God.

"Wow! Aren't you pleased, Mister Devil! It's a good sign for us". We waited patiently for the tempest to pass. When the rain stopped, our road now open, we started out for Arvaia.

Arvaia is twenty minutes away by road; it is a Turkish village or small colony which belongs to a landlord, the Bey of Arvaia. The village lies on open land, it is sunny, with one long slope towards the mountain and the way to Panaghia. On the left, a row of small houses all the same: stone walls, a roof of tiles, one floor, the ground floor, spaced between them. In every house lives a Turkish family in the Bey's service. Further on, on the right, are gardens, fruit gardens, out-houses, at the further end, the Bey's house, distinguished from the others by its height and large dimensions.

Between the two rows, a long and large stretch of land like an avenue, quite empty, goes from the valley to the mountain; up at the top of the avenue, an abundant fountain supplies all the village and Arvaia with its water.

The Bey received us on the first floor, in a simple room; simple, there was also furniture, all very clean. A door in the corner towards the gallery; in front, a European-style fireplace with a long mat before the hearth; a sofa on the right, aside the wall. The Bey was squatting down on his heels on the mat on the right side of the hearth on the gallery side. M. Binson, as a good diplomat, did the same on the opposite side. M. Jung and I, as strangers, sat on the sofa. M. Binson signalled to us to sit as he sat, but we preferred to look like barbarians and sit on the sofa. A lamp illuminated the room, a good fire was burning in the hearth.

We let M. Binson introduce us and start the conversation. We were frankish papaz (French priests); okoumoush! (learned), we had a big College at Smyrna. Me, with the white beard was the bash-papaz (the superior of) the College! The other with the red beard, was a teacher of sciences, mathematics etc. etc. a learned man!!! Binson himself, was our friend; he accompanied us to serve as interpreter. The Turk murmured his regrets at not being able to speak to us; he would like to listen to us speaking about science and wisdom. Meanwhile, he lit his long pipe. M. Binson took a cigar; between them a conversation started, half in Turkish half in Greek. They spoke about wise persons and wisdom; the wisdom of old times old time and the wise men of old.

I did not understand everything, but enough to follow the subject. Besides, M. Binson explained to us from time to time what was being said, also to make some joke in French without laughing, looking at the Turk with his face half-illuminated, quiet, unmoved, squatting upon his heels on his mat, his long tchibouc (long pipe) between his lips, an old man of another age; not Homer's Nestor, a patriarch almost like Isaac, like Jacob speaking with guests sent by God...

His speech was slow, quiet, measured; he stopped for a breath and meanwhile was smoking silently, puffs coming from his pipe. He spoke like an ancient sage, very little and in short phrases.

It was impressive; we would have allowed ourselves to be taken in by his charm, if we had not known who we were dealing with.

The old Bey invited us graciously to dinner. They brought the dishes in; fish brought in the morning from Scala-Nova, a friend of his had sent it. The old man said: "This is Providence;" I didn't know I would have the honour of having misafirs (guests), but God knew; he inspired my friend to send me this fish!!!"

A small table had been put between the hearth and the sofa. Everybody served himself. The Turk and the tactful Binson ate with their fingers. They gave us knives and forks. An occasion for another speech about old traditions, the ancient simplicity, lost in time. "Did our first father Adam use forks and spoons?" "Wasn't he happy? What need is there of all these useless appliances they use today?" and M. Binson approved... "What can we do? Today men with their pretend civilisation are not worth more than those of the old times. "etc. etc. M. Binson was saying that seriously, but from time to time he glanced at us after he had agreed with the old man.

After-dinner conversation was about old and modern times. As it got longer and longer without any result, I made a sign to Binson to broach the subject of our journey. He gossiped for a further ten minutes; finally he broached our subject to the old man. He became serious, listened solemnly and carefully, silently; later he assumed an air of astonishment, wordless, thinking, taking his pipe away from his lips, he answered that it could be discussed; he didn't say no.. he might be disposed..

....But there were many difficulties of all kinds... He asked finally for two weeks to reflect on the subject, to see things well... and put the difficulties in order! We made an appointment at Ayasoulouk, February 11, Wednesday, for a definite answer.

We left the Bey, thanking him for his patriarcal hospitality, wishing him a good rest, and left for the accommodation reserved for us.

It was one of the small houses described above; one square room and quite large; a brick-made ceiling, a floor of bare earth.

On this earth, a mat of straw two meters in size, laid next to the hearth. Was this the custom? Or was it the circumstance because of us? One door in the corner opened into the street near a small window; at the further end of the room, a fireplace and the hearth; at the sides jarricans, kitchen implements, gardening and workmen's tools; for light, a smoking lamp, illuminating or not..

Being the bash-papaz (the superior) I lay down on the mat in the first place, near the hearth, my head on my arm as a pillow, my body well wrapped in the mantle of Brother Verney, as a blanket... M. Jung lay close to me.. What a night!! They had sent the women elsewhere for the sake of decency, but the men remained and with them, a little child in a cradle. All through the night the baby kept waking up crying; one of the men had caught a cold, and was coughing and spitting... all night long with the sick man and the crying child.... nonstop. As soon as we closed our eyes and fell asleep, worn out by tiredness, the child's cries, the sounds of the men woke us up.

Just our bad luck, it rained hard the whole night. It was beating against the walls, the roof, the front of the house; if only that had been all, if only the rain had fallen outside!

Someone was moving nearby. I woke up, I looked. What did I see?

In the half-dark and hearth's light, Binson was sitting on the mat under the open umbrella. "What are you doing, M. Binson, instead of sleeping?"

"Sleep ..sleep! I should like to, but rain is pouring through and has soaked me!!"

Thus the night passed, between the baby's cries, the coughing man, rain pouring through the ceiling, outside and inside. Everyone kept his eyes open, all night long, awake since daybreak. We got up; we shivered, opened the door!.. Seven o'clock!

The clouds being low, the sky was full of rain and rain falling; a hard day started. What should we do? We had decided to go to Panaghia; but the weather!! Which way would we go? For one hour we waited, annoyed, wondering what to do, when at eight o'clock the sky became clearer. "Let us go up to Panaghia". Soon we got ready.

It was the first time I was going to Panaghia through Arvaia; the way was new for me, so attractive!!! In spite of the ascent, my heavy luggage on my back, my caouchoucked feet, well dressed, a heavy coat on my arms plus an umbrella, I arrived joyful. God blessed us, no more rain for the rest of the day.

It was the second time I had visited Panaghia; For M. Binson it was his first visit. Andreas was there; M. Jung was interested in the purchase and our projects.

We reviewed again what might be seen for the moment; later we went down on foot from Arvaia to Efesus, and back to Smyrna the same evening. With impatience we waited for the time proposed by the old man; fifteen days seemed so long!!

At the precise hour all of us were at Ayasoulouk. M. Poulin, Jung, Binson. While we were travelling by train, the old man arrived by carriage from Scala-Nova. I can see him getting down from the carriage, coming towards us without any hurry, his sad face a bad sign!

Well! What is the answer? It wasn't a categorical refusal but there had been more difficulties than he had thought. For the moment it was quite impossible to say anything. If you wish to come back again next week the same day, he added, maybe I'll be happy to give you a better answer.

Our return wasn't joyful. Meanwhile the old man hadn't said no; he had said come back again, maybe I'll give you a favourable answer. We hoped for this better answer, with all our hearts.

It had been decided to go back to Efesus the following week, but only M. Binson would come. If the answer was favourable, M. Binson would transmit it to us; if not, he had the mission to go around to see, to listen, to ask, try to find out with prudence as somebody had to know the real reason for it all.

M. Binson went back to Ayasoulouk and Scala-Nova. He met the old man again, spoke with some people, asked about the lawsuit, dispositions etc. etc. Finally, in the last week of February the answer was: "The old man wishes to sell, but he feels embarrassed because of his nephew, the lawsuit, and is unable to do anything; we must wait for the end of the lawsuit between the uncle and the nephew; to put it off until doomsday; what could we do?

February 27th, a cheque for 45000 francs was sent from Sister Grancey for Panaghia's purchase! With this capital we were able to buy; now we had only to wait, to hope for God's will, events, men's caprices and the favourable moment.

Five months have been gone by without any change in the situation. M. Binson was for waiting. "M. Binson, isn't it time to bring the subject up again?". "Not yet." How many times M. Jung, Sister Grancey, being impatient, asked the same question: M. Binson's answer was unchangeable: "No!". Even though I was quieter than the others, I found that time dragged... I pressed M. Binson:

"Stay alert! Keep your eyes open! Don't miss this opportunity.."

M. Binson was convinced, and believed, that it could take a long time to conclude Panaghia's purchase; thus, he suggested lending the 40.000 fr. instead of leaving the money without any income.

In mid-August I heard that some arrangement had been made between the uncle and the nephew. I knew also that the two lascars were looking for money at Smyrna; the one to pay the 2000 liras owed and get back his part of the land; the old man, to recover the difference and maybe acquire all the property. "M. Binson, they are looking for money! Isn't this the right moment?" "Not yet." "Keep your eyes open, don't miss the occasion!" "Don't worry; I'm keeping awake, I'll not miss this affair". Two days later, being ill, I left for Syria.

Some days after I left, Sister Grancey and M. Jung were not able to wait any more. They went to meet M. Binson. I wasn't there to calm them. "M. Binson, we must buy now; we must, absolutely must buy! What eternal regrets will we have if others buy this land!" M. Lobry, who came to replace me at the College and Mission during my absence, joined the movement.

He was satisfied to replace me at the Mission during my absence; he was also waiting for the purchase to take place. It had been decided; we should buy at any price.

Decision taken, M. Binson started to move. He met one person, he saw another; he gave to this one, he promised to that; of course things didn't happen by themselves! At any moment difficulties could come up, and many times there was a risk of failure. A share might have to be paid: to the Caimacam of 50 liras, to the President of the Tribunal another 50 liras, to the four councillors, 25 to each one to authorise the contract, to accept it for signature, to register. It has been necessary to buy subordinate employees whose help has been very precious at 8 liras; to reward some other friends whose zeal helped and contributed highly to this success; 50 liras.

When I got back from Syria, on October 20th, the transaction was under way. Some days later and all was concluded, but at the last moment an obstacle appeared. M. Binson, in spite of his ability and coolness, thought: "We have lost". He despaired for a moment; but soon he found his optimism and started the proceedings again. He paid some money and he became master of the situation! Finally, on November 15th, the feast of St. Eugene, my feast also, after the mass, at 8.30 in the morning, a telegram arrived at Sacre Coeur as follows:

Poulin, College Propagande, Smyrna. Scala Nova. 623 Nov. 14,5h 40 evening:

Congratulations, business concluded. Binson"

Doxa to Theo, It is done.

31.000 fr. total amount=200 liras to the nephew, 38 liras bacchich (tips), functionaries and mediators, 31 Lr. journeys, legalisation of the documents, sending of funds; 45 Lr. to the authorities, the last 800Lr. to the landowner for the purchase; total: 134 Lr, less than 31.000 francs in French money.

Maybe had we been less squeezed we could have saved on the price and bacchiches, which were enormous; but also by waiting further we would have missed the opportunity, and Panaghia would have been bought by others.

The purchase had been completed, that was the most important; the rest was simple detail.

The acquired land is by no means small. Its Length from East to West is 2 kilometres; and its width, 450-700-1000-1200-1300 meters, so that makes an average of one kilometre. Its total area is 139 hectares, 27 acres and a half or 1547,50 denums. It takes 3 hours to cross the plain, 5 hours with the mountains and the hollows.

It had been agreed, when the land was bought, to put everything together for our research; the Castle, the Terrace of Kara-kaya, Bulbul-Dagh, Kara-Tchalty and the Tower of a Hundred Guards, also the Grotto which is below, known as the Cave of Latone.

Also agreed on were clear and definite limits: the hollows, the peaks, the mountains, in straight lines from peak to peak. At the moment when the agreement was being drawn up I asked Sister Grancey: "In whose name will the property be registered? Do you want it in the name of the General Superior? Visitor of Province? The Superior of Sacre Coeur?". "My name" she answered. "Very well, my Sister, it will be registered in your name". It was done. It was logical, she had borne all the expenses and she still does for Panaghia: repairing the roads, construction of buildings, maintenance of the chapel, amelioration of the property, planting trees, annual expenses for excavations etc. etc. She has done this with endless generosity and good will. "Do make use of me, while I am here" she repeated often; "After my death I will not be able to help you".

Sister Grancey who had been wished feeling that she was getting old for two three years to leave the property by will in order that it would remain with the Children of Saint Vincent.

Before executing the transfer, we waited for the purchase of the mountain beyond the hollow in front of Panaghia. With the acquisition of the mountain we would have no neighbours, we would be completely on our own land.

As soon as it was known, the purchase of Panaghia caused some uproar. The Greeks of Smyrna were upset, they wished to buy Panaghia for their own Church. It was said they had prepared for this intention a public subscription at Saint Photini to collect the necessary funds, when they found out, alas, that as far as they were concerned the purchase had been done; those cursed Latins had succeeded in acquiring the sanctuary! They changed their tactics then; the watchword was saying- as the fox looking at the grapes had said- they had in any case given up the idea of buying, it wasn't important!!..

The Turks also reacted! "What! A land belonging to the believers!! Those French had taken possession of the heart of Islam!!...They got angry with the Bey who had sold it and threatened him, with the functionaries who had prepared and authorised the agreement; they were fired or transferred. They were against the Müdür of the Régie who had proceeded in our name to make the sale easier; he was sent off, away from Scala-Nova to Izmit.

They deeply wished to cancel the contract; they tried all ways for that. They even reached the Sultan. They tried to frighten Him, going on about strategic positions from where the French could observe and dominate the country... But as no war-boat, soldiers, nor bastion were seen, they renounced this War-mongering, as otherwise the contract had been well done. So whatever they did, they couldn't remake the contract. They accepted with resignation what had been done.

Today the Latin Cross shines on the pediment of the Sanctuary; at its side the French flag covers her with its glorious folds.

Chapter V

First Works at Panaghia. Material Works.

As for material works, there were four things to do at Panaghia:

1. To open up a road to get to it;
2. To build a house to live in;
3. To dig and find the Grave and all the rest;
4. To value the property and improve it.

I. The Roads.

The purchase was concluded on November 14th 1892, and certified on the 15th at Smyrna by telegram. Since December 1st they had been busy with the road.

There was access to Panaghia by four different ways: Kara-Kaya and the terrace; this was the way they used the first time, through Aziziye; through Arvaia; and directly from Ayasoulouk by a road crossing the plane diagonally, reaching the mountain a little beyond Lysimaque's Wall. This way seemed to be easier, shorter, more practical; they decided on this way.

Some months before, when a fire at Cavakli-Panaghia had burnt the whole side of the mountain, an old path emerged which led in the direction determined. To follow this path, we had to straighten it here, arrange it there, make it wider; in brief, to make it usable not for carriages obviously, but for donkeys, horses and simple pedestrians. Everyone was working with good will.

As it was important to finish quickly, a lot of workers had been hired from wherever they could be found, the railway, villages everywhere, 40-50 maybe more, 70 when needed.

To save the workers time on going home and back, they lodged them on the mountain.

Three big tents had been set up; one from M. Paul D'Andria, the two others from the railway. Every day a horse was sent down to Ayasoulouk to pick up bread, tobacco and other provisions necessary for the workers.

As soon as the workers started under Constantin Grollot's direction, a serious, very serious, difficulty arose, but it failed to stop the work because of the Bey of Arvaia.

We were owners of Panaghia-Capouli and perfectly free on our land to make as many roads as we wished, North, South, East in an area of one kilometer, but not beyond, because those were the lands of our neighbour. How could you cross your neighbour's land without his agreement? Fortunately, the Old Bey, although at first he protested, became quieter later, when he understood it was for his own profit for his property to be crossed by new roads, becoming more accessible, which would increase its value! He didn't protest absolutely! But he had one condition: to permit us to open up the road we wanted across his land near Ayasoulouk, we would make for his convenience a second road running from Panaghia-Capouli to his village of Arvaia....

It was an increase in expenses, ones which had not been calculated; but in this case we would have two roads to Panaghia instead of one; and we would be free to make roads wherever we wanted, over all the property. The Bey's request was graciously accepted; the men were divided to work in two groups, a big one on the road to Ayasoulouk, a smaller on the Arvaia road. Constantin directed the work with ardour. When on December 12th 1892, Sister de Grancey came up to Panaghia for the first time accompanied by M. and Mme. Borrel, Sister Thérése of the French Hospital, Messrs. Dumont and Poulin, we came across workers on the road and a part of the road already made. (M. de Montigny, Christian reporter from Paris).

There was something picturesque and graceful in the sight of these men spread out over the mountain, in groups or in teams, each group working in the place assigned; every group had its own tent to shelter in case of rain or tempest... But this pleasant sight of the mass of workers wasn't always so pleasing. M. Jung had more than one experience.....

On Sunday December 11th, the workers asked for permission to go down to Ayasoulouk, to the villages, to spend the day. M. Jung, who had just arrived, sensed the difficulty: "If they go down they will not come back!" To keep them, he called out to them:

"My friends; "he said", I wish for you to have a feast today in our honour; here are two kids, you roast them and you will have a good dinner. Here also are two jars of wine, you'll drink for my health! As for those who don't drink wine, I'll give each one 4 metals". "Viva the priest!" Nobody went down; they skinned the kids, put them upon the spit, when they were roasted they ate and drank to their heart's content. They were quite amusing, singing, dancing country dances up on the terrace near the Chapel, everyone was moving, jumping up, agitated by his own fantasy, one with a sabre, another with a knife, one with a dagger, with movements and menaces as if they were going to kill someone. "It was ghastly" said M. Jung, but they enjoyed themselves; and all ended well.

On December 21st there was an incident! Constantin informed us by telegram that the police had intervened. Armed policemen wanted to stop the work. Also they were looked for Andreas as the person in charge to arrest him and put him in jail.

For some days, a rumour had been running over the mountain. The Turkish authorities wanted to stop the work. Where did this rumour come from? What was behind it? Did the police want something? Were the people of Kirkindji the owners of the bottom of the mountain, were they against a new road across their land?

Whatever it was, M. Jung thought it wise to take the warning seriously. "Hurry up" he said, "We must finish the road to Ayasoulouk while they are still leaving us alone". Then he transferred the Arvaia group to the other, which was working on the road to Ayasoulouk, and they all worked on the same road to finish it quicker. Maybe it was this precaution which provoked the incident, or at least hastened it. The old Bey, seeing no workers on his land, thought he had been deceived. To complain and stop all of the work would be easy.

As soon as the telegram was received, M. Jung set out in haste to M. Binson, leaving two hours later by the eight o'clock train. They both went to Ayasoulouk. There they separated. M. Binson went to the Bey; if it was the Bey who was creating the opposition, he must take it back. If it was coming from the other side, the Bey had to prove his authority over his lands, and order the work to continue..

Meanwhile M. Jung had reached Panaghia to assure Andrea, Constantin and the workers. "There is nothing serious, nothing to make the police uneasy. All of you, go to work, as if nothing has happened. The rest is my business and that of the Consul of France," he said.

Later they met the gendarmes, the police, the chief-police, the Caimacam, to convince all of them to retract the decision taken, if a decision it was, or at least to obtain a delay. "If you want to stop these men working, then just try! They are Albanians, Montenegrans, Kurds, people who get angry easily! There are almost eighty of them! if you have an armed force to oppose them, then just try! If not, go away! They are poor people, they need to earn money; why are you disturbing them? They have no teskere? (permission to work). Oh! That is very easy to obtain. Do give us only eight days, and everything will be arranged".

Eight days' delay was obtained. What did our men do? Work on the road to Ayasoulouk was quite advanced. Quick! Constantin at once placed some men on the road to Arvaia to satisfy the old Bey...to double, to triple the team of men for Ayasoulouk, in order to finish the work during the delay.

It was done as decided: before the delay of eight days had ended, the road to Panaghia across the plain was completed. "Stop the work now if you wish. The road to Arvaia will remain unfinished, but it is not important for us..." They didn't stop at all; the second road was also finished during the week.

Two days later, there was a new adventure. M. Jung, as soon as he came back from Panaghia on Thursday evening, December 22nd, received an urgent letter from Constantin. It was then Friday 23rd, in the evening. The letter was full of alarm: "Come back at once! The workers are on strike; I don't know what to do:"

The next day, December 24 (Christmas Eve), M. Jung hurried up to Panaghia. "Why this strike? There must be a reason; what are they complaining about?" They discovered that Andreas and the chief of the workers, a Turk named Dede, had agreed together to extort out of these poor workers a half-copper per day for the bread and a half-coin for the tobacco they brought from Ayasoulouk. Two half-coppers made one copper per man; multiplied by 60, repeated 80 times every day made one medjidie, which the two fellows shared between them nicely! One worker spoke; a second, a third, a fourth; there was doubt. It no the reason for the strike, almost a mutiny. It was urgent to take a decision; M. Jung took it at once, resolutely.

It was late, and bad weather; he asked for a horse. A man had been wounded in the leg, had to be taken down. He took with him Pélécas, and both of them on foot, gun on shoulder, finally reached Arvaia. After a short rest at Arvaia, they set out again towards Ayasoulouk. It was late at night; it was raining; the roads were flooded, but nothing stopped them. In spite of his pain, the poor man on the horse took pity on them. "Take the horse, Mister". "No, my friend, you are hurt, we are not; and with the Lord's Grace, in spite of the rain, the dark night and bad roads we will get there.

It was 7.30 in the evening when the three men reached the hotel owned by Carpouza. In what condition though! Firstly they took care of the wounded man, they settled him down for as long as it would be necessary before it was possible for him to return home to Kirkindje. Then they thought of themselves. M. Jung had to take off his coat and waistcoat and the rest as well to dry them near the fire. Carpouza gave him a shirt so large it could contain a lot of men, but it was too short for M. Jung. They dried and warmed themselves. Meanwhile M. Jung sent for the chief of gendarmes to ask the price of bread and tobacco. He then informed him of what had happened up there and requested him to send four gendarmes at once if necessary, undertaking to pay the expenses involved.

Well dried and dressed, M. Jung was ready to set off for Panaghia's meadows, but the horse refused to move. They were obliged to get two fresh horses from Ayasoulouk. M. Jung and Pélécas mounted their horses and rode ahead in the night under the non-stop rain...

Arriving at the little inn by the fountain, they stopped to drink something hot. The owner of the inn, seeing they were ready to leave, asked if they were sane or crazy. "What are you doing on such a night and in such weather! One wouldn't put a dog outside!" "Rightly, it is because we are not dogs that we are going on our way." M. Jung wasn't so sure of his man, Pélécas! "Attention Pélécas! Sit firmly on your horse, keep close to me, neither too far right, nor too far left, or you'll fall into one of those holes". It was maybe nine o'clock. It was still raining.

Between 10 or 11 o'clock they got to the cafe at Arvaia; the door was shut, there was no light, the cafedji was asleep. They knocked, but not a sound! They knocked, they knocked, but in vain.

They went on knocking, with no result. They knocked and knocked, to no avail. They were going to break the door and shutter when the cafedji woke up. "Didn't we tell you to wait for our return?" "Who am I going to wait for at this hour, in weather like this?" "It's nothing to do with the hour and the weather, you must escort us to Arvaia village." "To Arvaia village! In this rain? One can see neither sky nor ground; the roads and holes are full of water, it's quite impossible!!" "Take your lantern and guide us".

Confronted by two guns and a giant who commands with high authority, the poor cafedji, who could have been frightened or something else, didn't say another word, lit his lantern, and set out in the rain..... Jung and Pélécas got off their horses-as a precaution- and followed him, walking on foot in the water and mud, pulling their horses after them.

Once at the village they gave half a medjidie as bachcich to the cafedji, who merited it, and sent him home to sleep; as for them, they went straight to Stelio's house, one of the workers who lived near the Bey. He was waiting for them. They knocked, at once the door opened, they were invited in.

It was almost eleven o'clock. Stelio had cooked a chicken which looked fine, but couldn't be for Christmas Eve!! Our men left the chicken for the yogurt. It was still raining...

M. Jung had decided not to miss his midnight mass; thus he was alert. He had to execute a project he had nurtured for many years; to look, if there weren't any more inscriptions at the Bey's place, for pieces of marble found at Panaghia.

Everybody was asleep in the tents, in the gourbi were Andreas, Constantin, Barba Photi; both the dogs were asleep and did not bark.

M. Jung woke up the men in the Gourbi: "At once," he said to Constantin, "Get everything ready for the Mass". Constantin took a box and put it against the wall; this was the Altar. While he made the necessary preparations, M. Jung changed his clothes, put on his cassock, and arranged his sacred objects.

The Mass began, served by Constantin. What an Extraordinary Mass! At the bottom, in front of the door was a makeshift altar; on the left was the fire and everything necessary for the hearth; on the right near the door was Andreas's bed, three horses and an ox looked on curiously... On the bed stood candles for the ceremony. In front were M. Jung's and Constantin's beds; near the beds, pressed close together, were Andreas, Barba Photi and Pélécas, full of respect. Above the priest's head a pumpkin hanging from the ceiling swung and touched his face every time he turned his head to say: "Dominus Vobiscum!" Outside was the rain, the two dogs, trying to get in to warm themselves, were shaking the door. Nobody opened it. They turned round, jumped on the roof and looked for a way in. Their large paws trampled the rotten straw; water was coming in through the holes; the poor celebrant did everything possible to stop this water dripping into the Chalice. How much all this made us remember the poor cradle of Bethlehem.

Midnight dinner was suited to the sanctuary's richness! A herring, and the remains of the sausage left over from 2nd December, when the Monsignor had visited us.

M. Jung woke the workers, who were sleeping, as we said, in three tents, twenty to a tent, with the chief of the group. "Tell them", he said to Constantin, "that the Priest has returned and he will give them justice". The workers in Constantin's presence got up. They listened to what the priest was saying, but instead of leaving, they stayed in the tent to chat among themselves.

Later, at 6 o'clock, M. Jung again sent Constantin with a formal order: "Get out." He was outside and waiting for them. They went out: "Wait here". When all of them were gathered, he spoke: Listen carefully Constantin, to what I am going to say; repeat it word by word to the workers".

1. "I don't allow anybody under my protection to be dishonest. Dede has cheated the workers; he will be sent away immediately."

2. "I want everybody to stay here today, I don't want it said that the workers went off displeased with us. Today they will go to the site, tomorrow is free for anyone who wishes to leave."

3. "Everyone must calculate what has been unjustly deducted; the same day I will repay it all. Now go. Nobody moved. I'm going to put a stop to this! Put them in line, and by squad. Good. Now, anyone who doesn't want to work, leave the line". Four workers left the line. These were the leaders, all good-for-nothings; one of them, an old robber said: "I keep these four men, you others go to the work-site". When the workers had left, M. Jung entered the gourbi and formed a tribunal, he, the great judge, condemning without mercy. On his right and left, seated like him, guns between their legs were Constantin, Andreas and Pélécas as assistants, if necessary executors....

"Bring in the first leader". He was the worst of all, a convicted thief. "How much do we owe?" "Six days"-"Here are the six days"-"My caution?"- "I will give your caution to the others; I am not obliged to pay you a horse every day to bring your provisions, and I am keeping a quarter more to reimburse my expenses. And now get out!" "But it's raining!" "Get out. I told you, take your mattress, your things and get out as quick as possible. If half an hour later I see you in the mountains, there will be a gunshot and the gendarmes will come. You will go through Aziziye. Go!" "The man bowed his head, took his mattress, his clothes and in less than half an hour, in spite of the rain, he had left for Aziziye. Since then nobody has heard of him.

"Send the second man in: Here for your six days, as for the caution, I keep it; I'm adding a quarter for my supplies. Go at once. You will go by way of Ayasoulouk, you will meet the gendarme and you tell him: "Here I am". He has to know you are not here anymore. Go! The same scene took place with the third: "You will go through Arvaia, don't miss the gendarme. When you get there, inform him you are not on the mountain any more."

The fourth came in, frightened, begging, beseeching, asking for mercy: Aman! Aman! "No, my boy! We have no need of outlaws at Panaghia". It needed a horsewhip to make him go like the three others, and take the road to Ayasoulouk.

After that quintuple "execution", discipline was reestablished. Nobody went on strike any more, but several times personal quarrels, violence, murder threats arose among this gang of men; and many times M. Jung had to intervene to pacify them and save the situation!

The men worked in fours; if one of them worked less, the other three turned on him: "Do you think we'll do your work?" etc. etc. A good worker among the loafers was injured this time: "What, are you our boss? Do you think you can command us?"

Sometimes there were only words or insults: "Loghia, loghia-words, words! But they were followed quickly by knives and murder threats. Five or six times workers ran away from the tents to escape the deadly strokes the others wanted to strike them. They fled frightened towards the Gourbi, where M. Jung received them as in a sacred place of asylum, until the anger was calmed, or he helped them escape without any danger.

In all of this, I admire Providence. Instead of an ex-officer, accustomed to use his gun, and to command with authority, a man who has seen war and is not frightened of battle, you put an ordinary man, a mystic, a giant like M. Jung!...Oh Lord! You chose the exact man for the position and the position for the exact man!

January 14th saw the end of both roads. The road to Arvaia as far as the fountain up in the village; and that to Ayasoulouk as far as the valley, in front of the sheepfold. The totals for the roads could be estimated as follows: 3 km for the road to Arvaia; 5 or 6, this beingfrom Ayasoulouk as far as the plain, not far from Panaghia-Kavak; thus a road of 8-9 km had been made on the mountain between December 1st 1892 and January 14th, 1893, by a gang of 50-70 workers.

Charges: 887 days and a half, 1/2 medjidie per day,

		francs:	1885,95
"	43 " " ", 1 medjidie	"	228,45
"	8 " masonry 1 "	"	25,50
"	43 " horses		
	provisions 1 "	"	182,95
"	buying and repair of tools	"	137,50
"	transport of tents and materials.....	"	48,85
"	M. Jung's journeys etc. lodgings, etc...	"	241,50
		Total:	2750,70

II. Houses and Constructions.

It was necessary to built a house at Panaghia; since the first day it had been agreed with Andreas, who was an old settler, to engage him to stay on at Panaghia, as a guard for the site. Andreas was a poor man, -as is known- who came a long way from Kirkindje to the mountain, every year at the same time to plant some fields of tobacco, and for that he was paying the old Bey of Arvaia regularily an annual rent of 45 medjidies. It was easy to convince him to do as we wanted; we told him to plant as much as he wished without paying any rent, so good luck to him! He accepted our proposition at once, happy to be employed under such good conditions as "the man and usufructuary of Panaghia."

From the moment we asked him to guard Panaghia, we also had to lodge him and his family properly; The hut of the old days, sufficient for a makeshift shelter, wasn't suitable for a permanent building. Moreover, our comings and goings on the mountain now took place more frequently and in all seasons.

M. Jung dressed like a farmer and could be accommodated in a hut, dating from the construction of the roads; but would it be possible to receive foreign visitors in this hut? Could we make the nuns sleep there? Or lodge the Brothers without light, furniture, among the hay, the horses and in the middle of all kinds of tools? No! We were also reduced, every time we went to Panaghia, to staying only two or three hours and returning to Smyrna the same day.

Did we need more time? We could sleep at the Hotel Carpouza, 7 fr. per person. Thus we went up directly to Panaghia, returned at twilight, slept at Carpouza's hotel, followed by a next-day visit to Efesus, went back to Smyrna; or we visited Efesus and the same evening we slept at Carpouza's; the next day in the early morning we went up to Panaghia and came down in time to catch the train.. It is easy to understand the inconveniences of both systems particularly in autumn and even more so in winter. Thus, it was decided quickly, very quickly, to build a house up there where one could stay as long as one wished.

Therefore, on January 9th 1893, even before the completion of the roads, it was decided:

1. A place should be fixed for Andreas, where he could set up at his own expense a makeshift hut.

2. A decent shelter should be provided for him and his family by the following autumn.

Projects; When we started their execution, political opposition arose which defeated our best intentions for a long time. We had not forgotten the bad impression left by Panaghia's purchase on the official Turkish Company.

"It is a Moslem land, and now these people are in possession of a centre in our midst".

M. Collaroa, manager at the Régie, had been exiled to Izmit because he helped with the contract; add also the Vali (provincial governor) of that time, who was an old Turk, one of the most fanatical. Afterwards we could not make the Government believe that we did not have hidden intentions, such as spying and delivering to France a strategic position from which to survey easily the coast, the sea and all the neighbouring countries. Thus, the police often came up to Panaghia, multiplying the visits to check if we were digging holes in the ground, building fortifications, establishing batteries, putting up cannon, etc. etc. It was said that a military commission would come up, check and be sure that we were not doing anything against the security of the state! "It is not prudent to ask for permission to build in such conditions. Be careful" said M. Binson to calm our ardour. "There is little you can do against fanaticism." He made us understand the best thing to do was to do nothing, to be silent.

Three months passed. January, February, March. In April the fanatical Vali was posted elsewhere. The situation looked favourable. M. Lobry was at Smyrna for the regular visit. M. Binson and I went to meet him. "Couldn't there now be some possibility?" "Yes, obviously!" We charged him with making all the necessary arrangements. He accepted, giving us cause for hope. "Eight days later," said he, "you'll have a favourable answer."

April went by, May, June, July also without any answer. Sister Grancey was impatient, M. Jung even more so. What could we do? I couldn't press M. Binson, nor require him to do more. Lately we understood the reason for everything being so slow; even we were no less suspicious. The Government was to renew an old law; it was forbidden to build outside the city without an "Irade". We had brought this about by buying Panaghia. The law was applied still at Gueuz-Tepe, Cordellio etc.

The law would be applied also for Panaghia, of course. What a nuisance!

All of the year 1893 was spent fighting officialdom; it was the same for the first five months of the year 1894. It was said on 30th April, 1894 that the "tezkere" had been obtained; but this was not delivered till May 14th. Finally we had recourse to the French Consulate. The Turks gave up; but not with good will and without bahchich! How many restrictions had to be accepted and signed as "sine qua non" conditions. It was prohibited to build a church, to open a school, prohibited to build any building exept a hut for the guard. The police had received an offical order to check scrupulously whether any of these prohibitions had been transgressed.

During these long months, waiting for negotiations, we were occupied with the plan; it had to include three conditions; economy, a suitable lodging, security. It not must be forgotten that the mountain had not lost its bad reputation, as thieves always settled up there.

A first plan, which was very' simple and practical, had been framed. There would be a long building with two large rooms on the first floor and two large rooms upstairs with a gallery in the middle, everyone having his privacy, but also the possibility of assembling in case of danger. This plan was refused, rejected as being too expensive. A second plan was prepared by M. d'Andria, Paul and Borrel, who were architects able to improvise. It was the same as the first, a little more modest, without the gallery. "Here," said M. Borrel, presenting me with his plan, "Here, this will be sufficient and just right, the cost will be a hundred liras". I couldn't help smiling: "A hundred liras for this plan! I am ready, dear M. Borrel, to sign at once a contract for 200": At that moment good M. Borrel did not want to believe me.

When the cost later increased by more than 100, later by 200-300 then 400 at last 500 Liras, he recognised that it was easier to trace a plan on a piece of paper than to be an architect and estimate the price.

The plan was accepted by Sister Grancey, who was in charge of the expenses, and later presented to the Turks. They refused the authorisation categorically. "This is a monastery you are submitting to us," they yelled. "How could we permit you to build a monastery on the mountain, considering the conditions up there? We are responsible for your lives, your peace of mind. If something bad happens to you, we'll be worried. No, no! only if you accept a troop of guards with you to protect you, at your expense of course." They permitted only a first floor with two rooms, without a gallery. We had to accept. Fortunately, when the building had been completed, M. Jung would know how to act.

M. Jung had left free the choice of the site; the house had to be near enough to the Chapel to keep an eye on it and to survey it; but also far enough -otherwise- not to lose the perspective. Since 27th of September, 1893, the day of the death of St. Vincent, M. Jung and M. Borrel had been up at Panaghia to make a preliminary study. After many surveys and long reflection, they decided on the site of the old gourbi, some metres to the rear.

Besides, for all that has been said until now, particular reasons had determined the decision to build behind the gourbi. They had all the stones there, ready to use and then to bring them easily for the new construction; they were situated in exactly the right place to channel the water of the fountain to the house, both for use in the construction and afterwards for everyday life. We will later see how Providence sent M. Jung to us, and also inspired us in choosing this site.

On Monday, 23rd of July, 1893, M. Jung came from Smyrna to Efesus, for he had to recruit workers and organise transport.

It was easy to recruit workers. Many of them had worked there during the roads on the mountain; they knew M. Jung and M. Jung knew them; one nod to the best ones and they hurried over.

It was different with the horse owners. Knowing its importance, they asked high prices for transportation up the mountain of the heavy material, they also found the proposed price very low. They took advantage by asking very high prices. They were malicious but there was a more malicious side to them! They were laughing at the Pope's embarrassment. When he found a solution, why couldn't he provide his own horses? Two horses cost 10 liras, he could resell them later for the same price at the end of the season. He decided at once. The beigirdjis (horse owners) stopped laughing when they saw our men setting off on our horses and leaving them. "Eh! kouzoum, do you still want five quarters for every journey?" M. Jung joked.

Saturday July 28th, M. Borrel joined M. Jung at Panaghia; the work of clearing away the ground, and making excavations started at once. M. Jung made the first stroke of the mattock; Constantin and his men continued.

These first tasks were so well done that on Wednesday 1st August, all was ready for the blessing of the first stone. I had came to Panaghia the day before with M. Thoillier. I blessed myself with surplice and stole in the presence of Messrs Jung, Vasseur, Thoillier, Borrel etc. etc. also in the presence of the workers, Greeks, Turks and others, to all of them we later gave, as we had to do, a bachich and a good drink to mark the occasion. Masonry work started on one side, in the meantime the ground was excavated.

All through the month of August the mountain was as animated as a bee-hive.

On the roads, donkeys crossed each others' paths, coming and going to bring bricks from Efesus at a quarter the charge, meanwhile horses went up and down for provisions and heavy materials. Diggers and masons worked on the site. Constantin, gun and mattock in hands, surveyed and commanded the work, he himself setting an example first. Up on the mountain, others were occupied in gathering pieces of limestone and bringing them to the kiln to be fired and ready for use in the building work. Those poor men!! They did not know how to distinguish between stones and stones... When we noticed it, it was too late!!! They had ravaged one or two pieces of Holy Cross Way, and brought them to the kiln to be reduced in lime!

Meanwhile, M. Jung surveyed the work and received with sweet cordiality the visitors who came up the mountain. There were more and more of these guests, some attracted by the work, others by the charm of the site. M. Jung was good to all of them, there was a place at the table for everyone, also a place in his dormitory.

They dined on the terrace on the North side of the Chapel in the shade of the plane trees. They slept under the stars, beneath the same planes. No sheets, no pillows, simple folding bedsteads, where everyone lay down rolled into a blanket. The trees served as rooms as well as coat stands.

On July 3rd, we went up with M. Thoillier to Panaghia. We were gathered on the terrace, about twelve of us, to dine and sleep. Messrs. Poulin, Vasseur, Thoillier, Borrel father and son, two Brothers from Samos-maybe three, plus Constantin and Pelecas etc. etc. Everyone had his place at the table and also his bed to sleep on. I felt very well in myself, and I was lying there when suddenly I saw M. Jung looking here and there, and at the trees, looking for something. "Where is my cassock?" and suddenly: "Oh! I forgot, I made a hammock for the Superior: that is the reason I feel so light...and comfortable..."

M. Jung knew how to encourage his men with his perpetual good humour and his endless cheerfulness. One should have heard him shouting: "Paidos" to the workers morning and night, for rest and meals. He congratulated one man for his strength and energy "Bravo, pehlivan!" He was one of his best workers, active and strong, ready for all kinds of labour. He gave bahchich for hard work, or an hour of rest after some effort.

With the guests it was all cheerfulness and continuous jokes to excuse our lack of facilities up there on the mountain. On 1st of August, at one o'clock in the morning, it became chilly; suddenly there was a voice in the silence: "Boys, shut the windows, it's getting cold!" The cold had woken M. Jung !!! Laughs from everybody at this joke; who could complain after this joke about the cold morning?

The food, as you can suppose, was not luxurious or varied; it was the same, same, and the same again...What did M. Jung do? The same as in high class hotels, where every day they give one the menu; he hung it up on a tree. Lunch: potatoes with bacon. Dinner: bacon with potatoes. Everybody was laughing, which made the difficulties easier to bear.

M. Jung, just as he knew how to be cheerful with his men, also knew how to be severe and maintain discipline as well. One day Constantin treated a worker badly. The same evening M. Jung reproached him for his unjustice. "If it is to be like this," shouted the angry Constantin, angry for being in the wrong, "I am going." He took his gun and went out. "Have a good journey, Constantin." But the fearful Constantin, when he found himself alone on the mountain, got frightened and came back in a hurry, very sheepish, and never referred to it again.

Another time, it was a Sunday, Andreas had been to Ayasoulouk to look for wine for the workers... At Eight o'clock Andreas wasn't back at 9-10 o'clock no Andreas. Finally, at 11 o'clock, he arrived cheery and unhurried, and went off to offer a drink to the workers camped South of the terrace of the Chapel, between the chapel and the fountain.

They drank and chatted, they drank some more, their conversation continuing; at last it went to their heads. Talking wasn't enough, they started to sing bandit songs.

M. Jung was annoyed. The uproar was getting worse so he intervened: "My friends," he said to the workers. "You are singing but you are not thinking of your fellows. You are disturbing them with your songs, you will wake up the good people who are sleeping on the other side of the chapel... It is late, tomorrow you must be at work early. Here! Drink a last cup, I'll pour myself, after that you'll go to sleep". He poured them a full beaker, after which they retired to sleep, saying to each other: "Kalos papas". (Good priest). But someone wasn't satisfied; it was Andreas. He felt offended and humiliated to be told off in front of the workers by M. Jung. He was drunk and he lost his self-control: "So it is you who are the master now, is it?" he shouted furiously at M. Jung.- "Si ise tora commandaris edho pera?"

He hadn't finished yet. Two strong hands like two hammers fell upon him, over knocking him over in the middle of vases, tenekes, pails and roots. He got up painfully, covered in bruises. For many days his wife had to massage him with embrocation; but the lesson served. Never did he ask again who was the master at Panaghia. Since then he had a respectful fear of M. Jung. "It must be like this with these savages".

The building was going well. It was the moment to add the necessary space and facilities that the Turks had refused. M. Jung easily added to the construction 3-4 feet more than was in the plan, raised the four exterior walls about two metres from the ground, to create between floor and roof a decent area good enough to serve its purpose. Nothing was visible from outside; nobody noticed anything. They made two dormer-windows at the extremities, for the moment it was just a loft.

Two or three months later, during the winter, when nobody is harassing us, we'll make windows, we'll put a ceiling under the roof; the primitive garret will become a small but real second floor.

By the time the construction was coming to an end, M. Jung had added a small addition to the rear to put hay and straw in, also to shelter the animals. The Turks protested. M. Jung asked politely: "Is it the law in Turkey to shelter men and animals under the same roof? Or leave horses, donkeys and oxen outside to be devoured by the wolves?" The Turks was silent and went away. M. Jung took care to reserve for the house a small room. It was the small room near the toilets, which is annexed to the kitchen and serves as a lumber-room. It is very useful. It remained to build an oven in local style, a fountain near the house and decent lavatories in order that the house became decent and possible to live in. Everything was done right under the eyes of the Turks.

September 16th, 1894: all possible work being completed for the moment, the house could be lived in. While we are on the subject of construction allow me to describe the chapel roof, the nuns' house, threshing-floor and barn.

The Chapel roof.

There was nothing more poetic than celebration of Holy Mass in the ancient Chapel on summer days, upon a rustic Altar, between half-ruined walls, the sky above our heads; but it was less commodious in bad weather, mostly during the winter's tempests and rain. After all, the old building had resisted so many tempests; but was it wise to believe that because it had resisted so much that it could also remain standing in the near future? This was as much for people's security as to preserve the building, so it was necessary to cover the chapel with a light roof; without changing the originality of the ruins it would be possible anyway to protect and preserve them.

Ever since the summer of 1894, when they had been working on the new organ's frame, Sacré Coeur, and the College yard, they were also working on Panaghia's roof. This work ended during the holiday, in case the Turks should arrive. Wood had been piled in the garret. It remained there until the end of August 1898..

It was the right moment, M. Jung thought, to risk -with some precautions and economy in our accounting- to risk building upon the two lateral walls of the center, some small columns of simple masonry, upon which the roof could be laid. The Turks had found out, for they had been observing us. "What, building! Of course not! As you see, only some stones to consolidate the house." However, we stopped. M. Jung did his best. On Sunday 28th of December he went down for his period of retirement. He did it ostensibly; for the season had ended. The police finished their inspection. M. Borrel and M. Barrelier remained up there to do some work such as replacing timber and covering it with a tarpaulin, in spite of the tiles. It took some days. When the police came up again, months later, all was done.

Turks and Greeks, as some said sent reports one by one to Konak. One day Kamil Pasha, with Said and his Brigade Major came up to Panaghia to see for themselves.. They looked and they saw.. "Are these the columns and the castle you say was built? Was it just for that you made me come up here? Leave me alone and don't disturb me any more..." "Thank you, Your Honour, for your visit and good words!".. We owe our freedom to them and we are very grateful to them.

The following days we covered only the middle, and left uncovered the Virgin's room. Two years later we also covered the Virgin's room. We replaced the tiles of the old roof, also the middle part.

The old, primitive altars were replaced by new ones made of marble, more suitable and nicer to look at; the bottom end of the Virgin's room was levelled and access made easier.

The roofing work on the Chapel alarmed Father Ensbach in Rome. He wrote to Sister Grancey on 10th of September 1898. "Allow me to inform you that I was troubled unjustly, maybe, by the news that they have built a roof upon the venerable walls of Panaghia. It seems to me it would have been better to leave them as they were, and shelter them under a large temporary hangar until it is permitted to replace this with a beautiful basilicata, including the Holy House, as for example Assisi, the basilicata of N.D. des Anges which keeps intact the small church of Portioncule. I am still alarmed by the horrors that have been committed to our sanctuaries in Palestine; St.Sepulcre at Bethlehem is almost unrecognizable." He also added: "Ah! How much more pious it would have been if the Calvary, if the Grotto of the Nativity had appeared to us after 19 centuries as they were in ancient times. I am afraid the same error could happen with Panaghia; they should expose the old pavement of mosaics, it is marvellous!!! Respect absolutely these old venerable walls as they are revealed by our Lord, through His servant of Westphalia, A.C.E. I hope the excellent M. Poulin will forgive these lines".

I hastened to reassure him as follows:

1. We absolutely shared his feelings and views.

2. We had been very careful when covering the primitive roof to respect the appearance of the ruins,

The good Father answered me with a letter full of joy:

"All you say me about the independent roofing satisfies me completely, and proves to me that this great relic is in good hands."

Rome, 20 December 1898.

I beg of our successors to read these observations and be fully penetrated by their spirit. As we found Mary's House, so we wish to hand it down to those who come after us. If ever the Lord gives us the possibility, our project has been decided long since: to leave the Chapel in its primitive condition and cover it with a big church, which will be the most beautiful and precious jewel.

Sister's House: - Once we had a house, we quickly grew accustomed to going to Panaghia and staying there. We Brothers slept, some up, some downstairs as they wished. As for accommodating Sisters and Brothers, we arranged this on condition that Sisters shouldn't be more than five or six in number. There was a common table when evening came, the men slept in the loft, the sisters downstairs, transforming the refectory in to a dormitory. If it were possible to have two houses! One for the Sisters, one for us!

There was at that time perched on a hilltop at Guez-Tepe a cottage made of wood owned by Braggiotti's family; the old family's chapel, which had also been Mgr. Marengo's old chapel when he stayed in the country, at Smyrna. M. Jung proposed to buy it, M. Braggiotti was ready to sell; the deal was done. On Wednesday 24th April, 1901 we were there to see if the cottage could be useful to us; on Friday 3rd May we bought it for a price of 800 Fr. On Wednesday, 15th May, M. Jung and M. Borrel went up to Panaghia, taking with them the cottage in labelled pieces. Together with them, Barrelier would reassemble the house and set it in place. It was a good aquisition. Buying it, taking it to pieces, transporting it and, putting it together again cost only 100 Liras. Really, it would be hard to own a house in the mountains for so low a price!

The Hangar: On 12th August Andreas's wife lit the oven to bake bread; suddenly a spark blew towards the stable, where there was straw inside and out. M. Jung could remember this moment precisely. This straw was too close!!! He was frightened of a fire; he would not give up until he had removed this danger. On August 21st he had the oven dismantled. Later, he had another one built, further away, on the opposite side, behind the House.

This precaution also seemed to him insufficient; after he had moved the fire away, he also moved away the straw. As soon as he had the possibility, he had a barn built some distance from the house. This would serve at the same time as a farm-yard. Only then did he feel quite reassured.

III. Excavations

Oh, the illusions of the beginning! C. Emmerich was so precise, we naively believed, and the Grave's discovery would only take a few days' digging. We were convinced now that unless there was a divine miracle or a fortunate chance, it would be quite difficult to discover it with simple excavations. After serious studies of the text, also the multiple excavations done on the mountain, we concluded that the Grave was surely on the mountain; the Grave was in the region of Kara-Tchalti....But where?... Upwards?... Downwards?... This was impossible to determine. Wisely, we took the decision to renounce our search until Heaven helped us, could we do otherwise? We hadn't the necessary permission, nor the necessary funds for a such a task, and finally, we didn't know where exactly to dig.

Even if we left until later the search for the Grave, we never gave up at the hope of finding it one day, maybe precisely when we were thinking about it less. While we were waiting, our activity should be limited to three subjects: to study the place. If there was a reason to dig here and there, it could be to clear up a particular point, to prepare for the solution of the problem, so that we could act without hesitation when the time came to carry out this particular excavation.

I thank the Lord for the facilities he accorded us to do as we wished in all these particular excavations.

In those days we had in our College many children and grand-children of His Highness Kamil-Pasha, ex Grand Vizier and the present Governor Vali of Smyrna; among these children was the Governor's last-born child, Sait Bey, It was easy to obtain a document assuring us the benevolence of the Police, and authorising us to dowse for water on the mountain. The Police had been warned, a hint had been dropped. They came rarely to the mountain or closed their eyes. What more could we ask? They let us alone, we profited from our freedom.

I'll not enumerate all the paths laid out on the mountain to facilitate further research, nor all the strokes of the mattock made here and there, to sound this or that rock which seemed to be of interest. I shall limit myself to the regular excavations, four in all. Two in the chapel, two around the House.

The first of these excavations was hazardous. In late July, 1894, they were digging the ground to the prepare the foundations of the new house, when the mattock struck a heavy stone. M. Jung examined the stone; without doubt, it had been put there by man's hand , and deliberately. "Well", he said to the diggers, "leave this place for the moment, work somewhere else and we'll look at that later." What was it under the stone? A grave? A hiding place? M. Jung wished to be alone until he was sure. He waited for the workers to go away, and then, helped by Constantin, pulled up the stone. Nothing but an ordinary wall was revealed. But a wall there underground was very astonishing! When the workers resumed their work, M. Jung ordered them to dig along this wall.... it was then that they discovered the two walls, well known, which border the front as well as the South side of the house today. Obviously there had been some ancient structure in this place. We noticed that the stone on the inner side of the breastwork was cut quite regularly, although on the exterior side a crude line seemed to have been made on purpose.

The stone overlapped the line. It was concluded that the ground outside reached the parapet; the inner side was a cavern or a hole. We found at once, in the centre of the two angles formed by the two walls, a big jar of terra-cotta used as a cistern; water pipes led to the jar. It looked like an ancient Atrium with a fountain in the middle. We decided for the moment to dig one or two meters of ground away near the mountainside, to reveal the walls more clearly.

On Friday 24th August, 1894 an interesting discovery was made. For three years we had been looking for the octagon described by C. Emmerich. On the other hand, I myself was in a personal difficulty, the more I read C. Emmerich the more I found the central niche narrow, seeing all that the niche was said to contain. Well, what had we just learnt from Andreas? Late on Wednesday 9th May, the floor of the chapel collapsed, revealing a large hole. Andreas had covered it while building a wall, building the niche and the circular altar. I was satisfied because this was the answer to my secret difficulties, but on the other hand I was disappointed, no altar, no round niche, no window; all that was Andreas' mark.

Preoccupied by such thoughts, also full of trust in C. Emmerich, I wrote to M. Jung: "Dig behind the chapel, you'll find the remains of a niche deeper than that one." M. Jung made them dig 0,50 cm. behind the chapel and stopped. "It is round, as you know." M. Borrel had to go up to Panaghia: "M. Jung didn't understand me," I said, "We must dig down to the old basement to find the old walls." M. Borrel passed this on. "Very well," said M. Jung, "I'll dig down to the basement", and started to dig again. What surprise, emotion and joy when at one and a half metres from the new soil, they found and revealed some Byzantine walls well, preserved... in octagonal shape!.. It was there that we saw the famous octagon; once more, the Visionary of Dülmen had been right.

This very appreciable discovery proved the octagon had been there for a long time, hidden underground. Nobody in the present century could have known about it, not even the local people, nor the workers who had built the new niche. They would have dug down as far as the original basement to support the wall, not let it seem to hang as we see it today. What about those who referred to Brentano and the others, who had probably visited Panaghia Capouli and knew about C. Emmerich, repeating all they had learnt from pilgrims?..

It was very beautiful, this discovery. People should see it, it should not be kept secret from people who visit Panaghia. Thus, two small walls to solidify the bottom had been set up; things were left as they were, to be seen by the public .

Tuesday 12th July, 1898: We started the third excavation. According to C. Emmerich's text, the Holy Cross Way starts behind the chapel, runs along the hillside, ends at Kara-Tchalti. We had been saying to ourselves for a long time that it could be possible, by digging a transversal ditch, to find the original Holy Cross Way. Thus, when this ancient road had been found we would follow it, getting firstly to Calvary and to the Grave later. After this reflexion, a ditch was dug.

Let us say immediately that the Holy Cross Way has not been found because they stopped before getting there, but many other things were revealed in the meanwhile that we had not even thought about! Here I copy from the Panaghia Diary.

14th July: Found the water pipe taking the water to the pool. July 19th. The first arcade appeared on the right beside an old supporting wall, behind the house.

We found two funeral lamps, plus a medallion with the head of Constantine.

July 19-22: Discovery of the lateral wall; a plaque of marble, perforated, from a fountain half-way up; an ancient step on the same side.

23 July- 17 August: Successive discoveries; behind the house, three vaults or arcades, followed by the first and second tomb, the second intact. In front of these vaults and at a distance of two meters, the remains of five columns and a thin slab of stone.

Under the third vault, 0,80 cm from the key stone a brick-lined grave, every brick 0,68 cm. in length, 0.49 in width; in the grave a complete skeleton, the head facing towards the chapel, the feet towards Kara-Tchalti, on either side, a body. In the hands, a medal of Justinian wrapped in linen. Collected among the debris were seven bronze medals, one of Constantine and another of Anastasius, pieces of funeral lamps, pottery, vases glass objects, tiles painted red and thick mosaics. On the path behind the House: well defined masonry, a step. On the right side of the house, in the meadows towards the chapel, jars were found in a water pipe. On the path, a bust in marble, a third of its natural length, badly damaged.

Excavations were continued in 1899, and finds were discovered, one after the other.

The discovery of walls like terraces, mosaics, a house in ruins, pieces of bricks, the remains of a funeral lamp, many bronze medals, and one urn with a child's bones in it, in the ground among the ruins. I must mention especially a mould in terra-cotta.

All these discoveries prove that the place was inhabited in ancient times. Was it an ancient Roman city as it would seem according to the Atrium, the remains of the colonnade and vaults, and the terraces found under the ground? Perhaps this city could later have been an Episcopate ?

Could it have been a monastery ? That was possible, judging by these remains, the grave, even the name "monastiri", which survived in local tradition. One thing that is important is: after the first successors of Constantine and even later, there was an important Establishment there.

August 1898; At the same time as the third excavation, a fourth was started, and as the second one was being done, a marvellous discovery came up.

I was taken ill at Panaghia. Before I was brought down in a hand-cart, held by four strong Turks, I left instructions to M. Jung to remove from the chapel all the remaining earth on the pavement, and to examine it. The men would clear the sanctuary entirely. As they were clearing away the 0.30 cm of earth which covered it, there came to light a pavement formed of small marble blocks, octagonal in shape, some intact, most of them in pieces. Today what remains can be seen, under the altar in the Virgin's room.

They dug as far as the wall which separates the two central rooms, exactly where C. Emmerich places the original hearth.

It was Thursday 24th August, the feast of St. Barthalemew, three o'clock precisely. In the same place, the workers had found some flagstones and pieces of marble; three were important, for they were blackened by smoke. What was this? ...One could say they were broken pieces of hearth. They called M. Jung. He was astonished. "Go on", he said. "Maybe we'll find out what this means."

They cleared everything out. Stones, stones, stones, about two cubic metres of stones...What a strange thing; only stones!.. Later we noticed they were white on one side, black on the other and had been placed, as if on purpose, in a hole dug in the rock, with pieces of bricks and coagulated ashes mixed with earth.

Suddenly M. Jung had an idea: "Not possible!.. What!.. Perhaps they are the stones of the chimney pulled down by the Apostles when the house was transformed into a chapel. They must have been buried there out of respect and a privileged member of our group has discovered them!" Those blackened stones covered in soot, those ashes, pieces of hearth, this hole dug as if on purpose, supported the hypothesis. At least there was no other one.

When the discovery was revealed, there were, apart from M. Jung, other attentive witnesses: two Reverends from an African Mission, the Reverend Mathiret and Fouquet, a priest from Paris, the Rev. Abbot Gouyet. They were so amazed by the discovery that they wished to write an official report immediately

The day after this memorable day, everyone was full of his discovery when M. Weber, learned professor and expert archaeologist, came from Smyrna to Panaghia.

M. Jung took a blackened stone and held it out to him: "What is this, M. Weber?" Weber touched, examined, smelt. "Soot," he said. "Are you sure ?" "Oh! There is no doubt". M. Jung held out the ashes to the expert: "And this ?" M. Weber examined, smelt, touched. "This is ash." "Are you sure ?" "Absolutely." "Well, M. Weber. Protestant though you are, I take you as a witness. We have found the remains of the Holy Virgin's chimney as described by C. Emmerich, which was removed by the Apostles or demolished to transform the house into a chapel, and the precious stones of which were hidden in the same place. We have found have them again after eighteen centuries!" M. Weber gave a muted cry of astonishment and said nothing. He had planned to dine with M. Jung, but he apologised and went away without dining. But the same evening one could read in Panaghia's Register Book: "I am back from Panaghia Capoulou, where I met M. Jung, who has discovered some really very interesting things." Written by himself were his impressions.

September 17th: Fifteen days later, our annual retirement ended and M. Jung went up to Panaghia to close the season. At the railway station of Ayasoulouk, he met a group of archaeologists, among them M. Weber, who had not been seen since 24th of August. M. Weber, perceiving M. Jung, approached him and spoke shyly, like a man when something hurts his conscience and he wishes to be free of it: "M. Jung," he said, approaching "I have thought about the recent discovery, about those stones that are black one side, white the other; there are similar ones on the mountain." M. Jung understood, and smiled: "Yes, M. Weber, they have found on the mountains many more like those stones, black because they are exposed to the sun, rain etc., white where the ground is; but have they found together with these stones soot, ash, pieces of brick and marble?" - "Ah sorry, sorry I didn't think of that". Then M. Weber bowed and went out. I never knew whether he tried to cast doubt on stones, ashes or soot after that day.

God Himself confirmed our pious belief, giving to these ashes of Panaghia the extraordinary virtue of healing; we shall relate further that they had authentically been approved by Greek, Jewish and Catholic doctors.

Here end all the excavations, approximately, done until today. We will wait for Providence to go further, for Providence to manifest Himself; We had a first sign with the apparition of the Black Lady, which appeared below Kara-Tchalti, and disappeared on a hilltop covered by cloud. A second sign appeared the following year on 15th October, when an extraordinary light shone for about ten minutes on the hilltop at Kara-Tchalti, to disappear suddenly, in the same place as the Lady in Black. We wondered at these signs, we thanked God; but we waited. He will show us more clearly the place where the Divine Virgin is buried, where to find Her Grave .

The important thing is, while we are waiting for this final sign, to create some facilities on the property to make it a lovely place to stay, and also for it to have its own income.

IV. The Value of the Property; improvements.

All our attention until now has been concentrated on four objects: Roads, accommodation, agriculture and the forest.

1. Roads.

Except for the two roads made in December, 1892, one leading to Arvaia, the other to Efesus over the plain, we opened up many paths across the property to make access easier. One from the Chapel to the Castle, one from the Castle to the southern boundary, one from the Castle to the big terrace at Kara-Kaya, from this terrace up to Bulbul-Dagh; from the hilltop of Bulbul Dagh down to the chapel. There is another at the end of the Holy Cross Way. There are four more through Kara-Tchalti: one crosses the road to Ayasoulouk and ends by turning Northwards to the station at Calvary: two climb directly to the southern side of the mountain and end there at the same point as said above. The first is called the Virgin's Way, the second, a little lower and parallel is called Gouyet Way; two others lead from the top: to the western boundary, which can be seen from the hilltop, the second leads a short way down the mountain to the road to Arvaia, not far from the hollow. There are paths as far as the neighbouring mountain, even though this mountain is not ours. We took advantage of the permission given by the owner to open up two paths from the hollow to the mountain, and we will make use of them until the mountain becomes ours.

All these paths must be maintained. They must be repaired every year, if not, they will disappear quickly, washed away by rain or covered by the leaves, earth, etc carried down the mountains.

2. Accommodation:

The chapel was roofed, equipped with altars, pews and other necessary things. The house has been furnished for the guard, and for ourselves. There is a second house for the Sisters with kitchen and outbuildings. We are thinking of building a third to lodge a couple; also a fourth one where some missionaries could reside permanently. Water pipes supplied these houses. Terraces were built in front, also pleasant gardens with the ground taken from the excavations and constructions. A small village was growing up on the site of the gourbis.

3. Cultivation.

It was possible, with water supplies everywhere, to establish a developed pattern of gardening; maybe later there will be an income from what is now surplus; but now there is no market, no way of selling, and high taxes, so they won't allow us to benefit. We planted trees. Tobacco was not sold any more. We had been planting olive trees for 4-5. years, about a hundred per year, but they need time to grow. We also tried some fruit-trees; will they grow and give fruit? Thought had been given to vines, but at this altitude ? We will try, the future will show us if it has been well done.

4. Forests.

Since we have been here, the forests have been our particular preoccupation. From the forest comes freshness, with the forest the mountain keeps its greenwood. This poor forest had been devastated. Before we got there the mountain was bare. Today we removed undergrowth to permit air to come through, also we planted traditional trees like the oaks of Bourgogne. We took precautions against fires; we kept at a distance everything that was harmful to the forest, particularly herds of goats, whose voracious teeth attacked the young shoots. The forest was not as it could be but nevertheless one could get some fresh air, as the trees slowly and victoriously grew in spite of everything.

Chapter VI

The First Historical Research

Meanwhile, M. Jung was occupied on the mountain with identifying Panaghia Capoulou as the position described by C. Emmerich, carrying out different tasks successively as mentioned above. We were also occupied with studying the question scientifically. Where did Mary die? What did the story describe? What was the value of our recent discovery?

Our first task was to refer to experts, to ask for their opinions. By the way, I also wrote to one of the best known authorities. It seemed to me that the most learned man to instruct us would be the Reverend Abbot Duchesne. My letter was dated 22 January, 1892, six months later after Panaghia's discovery. I described at length the history of the discovery according to C. Emmerich's directions. I described, with many details, the marvellous and multiple concordances, besides the site nearest to Efesus and I ended with these words: "We are poor men, not learned nor competent. Your Reverence, you who are learned and competent, what do you think of all this?"

The reply arrived without delay; it was dated 4th February, 1892, full of courtesy, but frank, clear and sharp.

Paris, 4th February 1892

To Rev. Poulin, Smyrna,

Reverend,

I would be very pleased to confirm your convictions and know you have found venerable structures. Unfortunately I can do nothing, and cannot say to you what I think of all that. Forgive my frankness and believe me, I would be very sorry if I hurt you!

"C. Emmerich's revelations are an abominable imposture. To whom does the responsibility for this intrigue belong? What is the measure of the self- proclaimed visionary and her accomplice Clemant Brentano? Do they share the equivocal merit of having compiled apocryphals, Gospels and lying legends? It is not for me to explain and I think Time should be employed for more useful things.

"Even if we take for gold what is mere lead, it would not be difficult to prove: the indicated place is not where you have stopped. I have before my eyes in German the original text of these beautiful visions; it seems the mountain where Mary dwelt is near the Jerusalem road; that means near to Aidin, three and a half hours from Efesus. If this is not the case, it is marked on the map brought to me from St. Lazare; it is in the neighbourhood nearer to Efesus."

"It is said also: the hilltop is behind the house, nearer to the sea than Efesus. Efesus is many hours' journey from the shore; here is the mistake. Whoever wrote it doesn't say that in those days the sea came nearer to Efesus, which was a city with a sea-harbour. The visionary describes things as they were in the year 40 A.D. She should purge herself of such lies.

"The photographes represent the ruins of a small country chapel, like many others in those countries. The building has no definite style; it could be 12th century, or 6th. I hope the young men who told me didn't recognise there "at first glance a church of the Ist century", otherwise I should conclude they have permitted themselves, although it is impolite to say it, to play a joke on you.

"As for the Holy Cross Way behind the house, it makes me remember these pictures where the Holy Virgin is seen in the scene of the Annunciation a rosary in her hands."

"In things of this kind, instead of listening to false prophets, one should consult the traditions and look at Efesus not as the Holy Virgin's House, but the sanctuaries of St. John, St.

Madeleine, the Seven Sleepers and St. Timothy. These were visited during the Middle Ages as a holy place of Mary, (out of the Church, extra-muros), whose name is more a problem than a precise indication. The Middle Ages are completely mute. They have been leading us to Jerusalem since the 5th century. Visionaries have tried to profit from this tradition, but their malice is detected."

"Forgive me, Reverend, for speaking like this, I am a Breton, I call things by their name, a cat is a cat. Otherwise my religious and ethical conscience obliges me to protest against the establishment of a sanctuary under these conditions. I should like to ask St. Paul's oratory to beg you not go to further and not to expose our Brothers, your Congregation and even the Catholic Church to the well merited sarcasm with which they would receive your discovery.

I suppose you are more captivated than convinced. For God's Love, be strong and resist.

Receive kindly, Reverend Father, all my deep respect. 36, rue Vaugirerd.

Duchesne

Meantime, the Rev. Abbe sent me this letter, he sent another to Reverend Fiat Superior General as follows:

To Reverend Fiat
Paris, 5 February 1892

Reverend Father,

"I think is my duty to call your attention to the discoveries recently found near Efesus, and the unbelievable condition of spirit your Brothers are in. One of them, M. Poulin, (if I read his signature correctly) referred to me for this purpose. I replied to him in unfavourable but generous words.

"At first it seems to me very imprudent to use C. Emmerich's revelations as those Reverends are doing. These revelations are a certain imposture, the product of lack of concsience. To introduce such utterances in traditions and archaeology is an error. It is a characteristic wrong step. If publicity ensues, sarcasm will fall upon the Lazarists of Smyrna; it would be regrettable for these Reverends and it would be an injury to their reputation: until no they have represented w Catholicism and France with dignity in the Orient.

"I remain at your disposition, Reverend, for further information, in case you wish to ask me.

Receive please the expression of my respectful consideration, in Jesus Christ.

30, rue Vaugirard, 5 February 1892   Priest Duchesne

M. Fiat hastened to sent me this second letter of M. Abbe Duchesne, also enclosed was a note from M. Pemartin, General Secretary, with his own visiting-card.

The note was like this: "After my long interview with the Reverend Duchesne, I firstly thanked the eminent professor for his letter to the Rev. General Superior for the trouble he took to write. I strongly affirmed that the Rev. Superior and his council, ever since the beginning, have opposed time being spent on the supposed discovery at Efesus, and they didn't place any trust in the reports on this subject.

"Rev. Duchesne explained himself; referring to the thesis of the Reverends, politely and with courtesy. He said to me that he had read again on that occasion C. Emmerich's text, and even wrote to the School of Athens Director, in order to know their opinion. They have visited the place with Rev. Poulin. It gave me the opportunity to cast light on M. Jung's antipathy to visionaries, and mystic phenomena.

"I expressed Rev. General Superior's wish that this should remain private, not thrown by some indiscreet communication into public dispute, favourable or not, in historical and scientific periodicals."

As for the visiting-card, it was white. I interpret it like this: "You see my objections against your enterprise; be careful, all of you... I won't impede you; but be prudent; avoid compromising us."

All this was not to encourage the discoverers, particularly the Rev. Duchesne's letters; but as we were for verity and right-ness, we were neither troubled nor upset. After mature reflexion, a strange thing happened that might encourage us and become a reason for trust. Firstly, why this letter of Abbe Duchesne to the General Superior? Why this passioned opposition when we had behaved to him so honestly, as simple persons, without any pretensions, as people who do not know and ask to be informed?? It seemed to us there was something suspect and selfish under it all. The professor's allegations made us think; how could we treat as an "abominable imposture" C. Emmerich's revelations when, for the past six months, we had constantly established their accuracy! To claim that Panaghia was not the place designated by the visionary, to us who we were actually there and could see with our own eyes!!! Finally, to declare that C. Emmerich was not inspired, would never have stated that Panaghia was nearer to Efesus than to the sea because Efesus was a sea-harbour... It is not the vision that is wrong, it is the dear scholars! Yes, Efesus was a sea-harbour in the Holy Virgin's day, but by a long canal, of which traces remain.

These remarks and others as well urged us to reflection. Such an important subject had not been studied seriously.

It was right, as we knew later, and became convinced in our subsequent observations.

We were there, when summer came, but an attack of tiredness obliged me to take a complete rest. I made use of this obliged rest to do two things, to have a change of air and go to Jerusalem. Everything I saw in Jerusalem, everything I heard, fortified my belief in Panaghia.

Ever since I have studied this historical problem, I have started to have an urgent feeling about the report, that there is no basis for the Jerusalem tradition. I also perceived, moreover, that those who favoured Jerusalem all copied each ather with a deplorable instability; they all turned to Juvenal as the ultimate authority. Juvenal, always Juvenal; should Juvenal be the first to put Mary's Grave at Jerusalem?. On leaving the Holy City my doubts became certitude.

During my stay in Jerusalem I had the opportunity to have every day as guide the renowned Brother Lieven; "Brother Lieven, what is this column that I see against the wall?" "It is a souvenir acquired when bringing the Holy Virgin's body from Sion to Gethsemane. A Jewish priest rushed upon the man, telling him to throw it down, and he was punished on the spot by having both his hands cut off...." "For what reason?" "That column against the wall!!" "But the wall is made of dry stones and quite recent isn't it?" "Obviously". "This column, when did it get here?" "I don't know or when I say I "I don't know" Do you understand?" - "Yes, thank you Brother".

"Brother Lieven, does this church dedicated to the Virgin have a small share of pilgrims' devotion, or of the people of Jerusalem? Whose are these graves on the left and right? Under the steps?" "St. Joakim's grave, St. Joseph's grave, St. Anne's and the grave of a Christian princess." "Oh! Brother, all these graves together! Gathered in a structure of the 11th century. What an opportunity! How could one admit such a thing?" -"I am telling you what I was told, that is all." "Thank you, Brother...."

Later we talked about Panaghia. "Do you know, Brother, I have started to believe seriously in Panaghia. The more I study the less I find in Jerusalem's favour; there was nothing in favour of Jerusalem before Juvenal: no Father, doctor, historian, writer, pilgrim, no-one.. Juvenal, always Juvenal; before him there was nobody, absolutely nobody. "Pardon, Reverend you are wrong". - "If I am wrong, I ask sincerely to be instructed; who do you know of?" "There is St. Epiphany, take my book!"

The Brother took it, opened it at an article about the Grave, and pointed with his finger to the first line "Look," said he, "St Epiphany" "Very good, Brother; but look also at the reference; put aside the name of St. Epiphany and read down to the corresponding note: as Juvenal says!" "That is right," said the good brother, surprised," I didn't notice that". He soon added very honestly, that he, too, was searching for the truth, he could support the Panaghia thesis as soon as his mind, which was not opposed to it, could be persuaded that Panaghia was the stronger possibility.

Meanwhile I wished to be informed about Jerusalem, looking at the monuments, studying the exhibits, asking people, listening to arguments and objections. M. Dumond, who was recovering after a long illness, had gone to Vichy for a long rest. For the rest of the season, he stayed at the Main House, preaching about Panaghia, and on this occasion defended the case like a valorous knight. He did better, he searched carefully and with ardour in the great Library, reading huge volumes, copied the Fathers', Historians', Pilgrims' notices and brought on his return a rich collection of documents, authentically witnessed.

Dear Rev. Dumond! One more who served Panaghia!. Apart from that, all I have reported, there are many lines, papers, pages, and copy-books, all composed by his artistic pen to honour Panaghia. How many convincing speeches filled with ardour did he make for the victory of his cause! Also, how ardent were his prayers for the Discovery of the Grave we all yearned for!

May his modesty not be shocked by such just respect! Did Jesus say: "Dicite justo quoniam bene... Tell to the virtuous what is good". I am doing nothing else at this moment: O Mary! Bless him as Yours because he is really Yours, he worked and he works with urgency devotion and constance for Your glory!

From the documents collected in Paris by Mr. Dumont, and those we could find at Smyrna, too, five things seemed to emerge clearly:

1- There is no known authentic authority for the Jerusalem thesis before the 4th century

2- The first Fathers of the Church, who talk about Gethsemane, hesitate, and all they know is through the apocryphals.

3- In favour of Efesus: the best authors of the 16th-17th centuries: Cornelius a Lapide, Tillemont, Ruinartserry, Dom Calmet, Baillet, Bible de Vance, Benoit XIV etc. etc. ...

4- Recent authors and historians are divided, half being for Efesus, half for Jerusalem. They refer to the two opinions without pronouncing any.

5- From this context, a conclusion emerges: Efesus overtakes Jerusalem, and looks like winning.

We had well worked that year, 1892. M. Jung was up on his mountain, researching and studying texts, when an event that was pleasant and unexplicable shed new light upon our work and what a light!!

M. Binson, during his comings and goings in connection with Panaghia's acquisition, had many opportunities to meet Mr. Constandinidis, Mayor of Kirkindje. This gentleman, who was learned and a barrister at Konak, in Smyrna, told M. Binson something strange one day.

As he said, the people of Kirkindji had known Panaghia-Capoulou since time immemorial. They had always greatly venerated it and had never missed their pilgrimage are every year, the eighth day after the Dormition, in memory of the Holy Virgin, who as their fathers believed, must have lived and died up there and they were also sure that Her Grave was up there, too.

How did these news affect us? The people of Kirkindji are known as being the descendants of old Efesians, the heirs of their traditions. What a strength for us if the claim of Kirkindje's mayor could be proved and testified! Thus, as soon as I heard about it I took the precaution of first making sure of the fact itself and later to obtain if possible an authentic attestation.

M. Constandinidis cordially accepted my request to serve as intermediary between me and his compatriots. I set up a very simple and calculated questionnaire designed not to inspire any inclination towards Greek fanatism, while giving us plenty of satisfaction on the points we wanted to clarify.

M. Constantinidis carried out this commission with good will. He soon gave me a document properly signed, properly paragraphed, attesting all his village's belief in the death and assumption of the Holy Virgin at the place known as Panaghia-Capoulou... Everything is entire, exact, in its original from, that in spite of the great publicity given to this witness, no opponent for ten years has dared to cast the least suspicion upon this document in which questions and replies were properly translated from a Greek mixed with Turkish.

Questions and Replies

l. What were the origins of Kinkindji village?

R. Kirkindj village was established by seven slave families after the fall of Efesus. These seven families, escaping from the Turks, took refuge up in the Efesus mountains around the city, looking for a place to hide.

They had chosen this place as being far away, and settled down.

Later the Turks, on meeting these refugees, asked them about the place where they lived. They answered: "We live in a place where the water is good, the weather is good but the soil is infertile. "suyu güzel, havası güzel, yer biraz çirkince", where the name of Kirkindje came from: tchirkindje.

The village has been in existence for about 200 years. One century ago, only eighty houses existed, today there are one thousand and thirty.

2. Where do they consider St. John's Grave to lie?

R. to the West of Efesus, on the mountain known as Sevgili-Dagh "lovely mountain" near the Efesus Agora, today known as Sirevler, one hour's distance from the railway station.

3. Where is St. John's church?

R. West of the railway station, twenty minutes from the Castle gate.

4. What do people say about Kriphi-Panaghia?

R. After Jesus' crucifixion in Jerusalem, Our Lady Virgin Mary, God's Mother, was under the care of St. John; they came to Efesus. The Virgin made a grotto west of Efesus up on the mountain known as Boudroum. This dwelling was a half hour journey from St. John's Grave, and one and half hours from the railway station. Because of pagan persecution, the Virgin was concealed there; they called this grotto: "Ghizli-Panaghia" or Kriphi Panaghia, (Hidden Virgin). They celebrate her feast on the day of Zoodohou Pighis "Spring of life", the Friday after Easter.

5. What do they say about Kavaklı-Panaghia ?

R. The Holy Virgin, because of pagan persecution, left her hiding-place at Kriphi Panaghia and went one hour southward to a place called Kavaklı.

At this place, as today, there were planes, poplars and thence the name of Kavaklı-Panaghia. They celebrate 24 of November, Presentation Day. This place is one hour and a half away from Ayasoulouk Station.

6. What do they say about the Holy Virgin's stay at Efesus?

R. They don't know anything about it.

7. What do they say about Capouli-Panaghia ?

R. The Virgin left Kavaklı-Panaghia. She fled Westwards. Bulbul-dagh, "Nightingale Mountain" which is two hours' distance from Ayasoulouk Station. It was there, in her home at Capoulis where her "Dormition", took place, which they celebrate on 15th August.

8. Since when have people lived at Capouli-Panaghia? Did foreigners ever come to visit the country? Was that the place they went to?

R. Whatever is known about Panaghia-Capouli is known by the older generation. An old man ninety years old testified and he said the Holy Virgin and God's Mother's Grave was at Panaghia-Capouli and he knew it. He said also that "Ayasoulouk" means holy water-Ayasma. They said then, as today, that the pilgrims' place was here as well.

As for travellers to Capouli, they had not seen any for thirty or forty years. Strangers came to see the Theatre, Diana's Temple, St. Paul's Prison, the Agora but nowhere else.

9. Apart from Kriphi-Panaghia, Kavaklı, Capouli-Panaghia, is there other church dedicated to the Holy Virgin?

Apart from these three sanctuaries , there are at Efesus and in the vicinity about thirty-three churches or sanctuaries. This information was given by all the village of Kirkindji. In consequence, I, the undersigned, descended from these old families of the said village, recognise the authenticity and perfect truth of these answers and I assume all responsibility.

Done at Kirkindji, 2/14 December 1892,
M. Constandinidis

Thus the Kirkindji tradition was for us, and with the Kirkindji tradition, that of old Efesus.

If this was not true, where did this particular belief of its people come from? What the people of the region and his own clergy placed at Efesus, he placed at Jerusalem.

Feeling strong with all the results obtained and wishing to clear up the question completely, I referred again to M. Duchesne, asking him to do two things:

1. To indicate better reasons against Efesus,

2. To help us to explain the marvellous similarities we had established between the descriptions of C.Emmerich and Panaghia Capouli itself.

Either M. Duchesne should succeed in giving us a decisive reason and satisfying information or he should be silent.

If: 1. We have to accept defeat, and we honestly decided to do so, why should we resist reason ?

If: 2. Our victory is sure. Should I say that I expect more from the second hypothesis than the first ?

The reply of the most learned scholar was more pathetic than I expected.

Ad. I. All these objections led to only one conclusion: there was a total absence of tradition about Efesus .

Ad II. No concordance; nothing to explain. I limit myself for the moment to summarising these two letters. They will soon have both of them in extens, in my reply to M. Allou.

So what! So that is all High Science had to object against Panaghia? Without similarities, without traditions?...

After such a reply, I didn't doubt in the final triumph of our case; most of all I was feeling strong, very strong, against our friends and against our enemies. Poor M. Allou, my old professor of Sens, today Assistant of the Congregation at the Main House, was the first to suffer from the experiment.

M. Allou, witnessing Paris' distrust of Panaghia and sharing these opinions himself, supposed it to be a duty, on his card of January 1893, to add to his New year Greetings this small, friendly warning: "I am sorry to know you are involved in this action". He attracted the following reply:

Smyrna, 8 March 1893

Sir and Very Honoured Confrére

May Our Lord's Grace be with you forever:

"Thank you for your small word and fatherly advice concerning Efesus. I understand and accept it as given by you. However, let me tell you this: if I were in Paris, not seeing what I see, not hearing what I hear, very probably I should think as you do. But if you were in our place to hear what we hear and to see what we see, and most of all to see what we see, I consider strongly that it would be hard for you to not think as we do.

In his last letter, Reverend Father says that one of the reasons he ascertains in you is M. Duchesne's witness against us.. For a while I had the urge to write to Abbé Duchesne and request his help, his light. Would you mind if I let you know any subsequent requests and replies ?

Hereafter my letter:

Smyrna, 2 February 1892

Reverend,

For some twelve or thirteen months, I have had the honour of writing to you about some Ruins searched for and found in the vicinity of Efesus, according to C. Emmerich's indications, also about the Holy Virgin's House at Efesus. I had asked you what your opinion was about this discovery. You replied to me sharply and sincerely, I thank you. You would make me pleased, very pleased today, if you would have the kindness:

1. To give me the best reasons known against the Holy Virgin's stay at Efesus or in the neighbourhood;

2. To help me to explain, with good sense, this brutal fact: how C. Emmerich, who died in 1824, could have so minutely, and exactly described in terms of position and plan, an old ruin lost in the mountains, unknown by the learned, unknown by the pilgrims, and which of course, she had never visited herself? If she had copied some document, where is this document? Is there a forger who added to C. Emmerich's work? Who is the forger? What is his interest, his goal? And where could this forger have himself imbibed this information, providing a description, so exact, so detailed and and at the same time so perfect? And all this when, on the testimony of all the people who live up in these mountains where until the last fifteen years, nobody except a lone shepherd could have ventured without the risk of being killed, kidnapped, mutilated by bandits?

I do not doubt that with your vast historical erudition, you will be able to explain, to answer all these divers points, to satisfy me. In doing so, you will do a great service not only to our humble servant, but also, I dare say, to all of Smyrna, which today even is interested in the question. I have the honour to be, etc. etc.

Here is the reply
Paris, 12 February 1893

Reverend Sir,

I have told you it is impossible to introduce to a serious debate a book like C. Emmerich's visions. Archaeology relies on witness, not on hallucinations. Besides, having seen the plans and photographs you sent me, the similarity you claim does not exist at all. I could not come back again at this point without the photographs and plans, which I gave back to the person who brought them to me.

As for the reasons for contesting the Holy Virgin's stay at Efesus or in the neigbourhood, there is only one: a total absence of traditions. After the Council of 431, one church of the city was named Maria; one of the documents issued by the Council describes Efesus; this is followed by a reference to St. John and Maria... after which, the phrase is interrupted without it being possible to say how it ends. After that, all documents we possess about sanctuaries are absolutely silent.

The church named Maria, which seems to have been a Cathedral, could have changed name. Pilgrims visit the sanctuaries of St. John, the Seven Sleepers, the 300 Fathers St. Mary Magdalene, and of St. Timothy. As for the sanctuary of Mary they have no notion about it. There is mention of the Holy Virgin's village, which served as an argument against the Nestorians of the Ecumenical Council. If you take a glance at this, the tradition of Jerusalem is so manifest, so well proved that there can be no hesitation. This objection has been rejected by the visionary or the editor of her dreams. They imagine an explanatory system, but the ruse is evident.

Under these conditions, I can only renew my objections and prayers of last year. I am sure you are on the wrong path, you are wasting your money, and you give to the piety of believers an absolutely erroneous direction. This does not mean you will not succeed; it would not be the first apocryphal sanctuary to be established. But my duty is to protest strongly.

Please would you accept, etc. etc.

L. Duchesne

You have read in extenso the questions and replies. Now judge! My letter is clear, my questions very precise. I begged Rev. Duchesne to give me the best reasons he knows against Holy Mary's stay at Efesus or in the neighbourhood.

How does he answer? "All reasons lead to only one: a total absence of traditions

I repeat again: if there is no tradition at Efesus, how, therefore, did this controversy, which nobody has been able to resolve for centuries, arise in the first place?

"Why did Benoit XIV, student ex professo, to the question "inse" allow the indecisive and personal feeling he declared for Efesus?"

"Why, of the visitors, is there one half in favour of Efesus, the other half in favour of Jerusalem and those who hesitate between two cities?

"Where did the belief of the people of Kirkindji and the vicinity that the Holy Virgin died and came to life again on the mountain known as Bulbul-Dagh come from? Why have pilgrimages been made since time immemorial to Panaghia-Capoulou, particularly to celebrate the Assumption?

I beg the Rev. Duchesne to have the kindness to help me to explain logically the perfect similarities existing between C. Emmerich's description and the ruins we have before our eyes. To explain this similarities would be difficult for someone who sees only in the visions of the German ecstatic sometimes a joke, sometime dreams and hallucinations. He denies it all. The similarities do not exist.

I beg a thousand times the pardon of the well-known and learned Master... Who will he convince from his office in Rue Vaugirard, thousands of miles away, with simple plans and fotographs on his desk, that he sees better than we, who are actually here? Also, so many people who are by no means stupid or blind, men of high society, men of the church, writers, reporters, tourists, engineers, architects, naval officers etc. etc. saw as we did and confirm there is complete similarity.

"To the complete silence of Efesus we opposed the manifested and proved traditions of Jerusalem". Yes, let us speak about these famous traditions of Jerusalem; a column, a grave, a rock. The column: it was there that a prince of priests threw himself upon the Holy Virgin's coffin during the funeral procession. He lost at once the use of his hands but he was converted and found again the use of his hands, says the legend. The grave: it is there Mary's body was laid after her death. The rock: St. Thomas was there when he saw the Holy Virgin rising up towards the sky."

"Very good! It is decisive! It is said that before 452, (that means before this forger Juvenal) that nobody knew, absolutely nobody knew anything about this column, this grave or the rock. St. Paul said nothing, nor did Sylvia, the pilgrim from Bordeaux in 333 who had visited the country (310-403). The good Father, who doesn't know even if the Holy Virgin is dead, if she is buried. Not one of her contemporaries required such information. So what about this burial, this column, this rock? Of course it is legend! You conclude from all of this that the Efesus tradition is to be rejected. There is something "minus rectum" to reject without studied it".

"And now, Reverend, a word to finish. Do not think we are fumbling in the dark as far as Panaghia is concerned. Neither M. Vincent, M. Portail, nor M. Jung, even less I, your servant. God prepared everything "ab ovo"; God guides everything. It precisely because we have seen God's signs in Panaghia that we have given ourselves to this task, to serve Her better. "A Domino est istud, et est mirabile in oculis nostris." I see with peaceful eyes all difficulties that would come by man or things "The stone is detached from the mountain, nothing could stop it rolling down."

I remain your respectful servant."

These last words of my letter explain our feelings sufficiently since our research. We believe in Panaghia humanly and divinely. Humanly because of the weakness of the opposite thesis, which was every day more obvious; divinely because we touched, we saw, we felt God's hand in this fact.

From there comes this self-assurance, which will manifest itself henceforth in all our writings and conversations. God is with us, who can stop us? If God is with us, who can be against us? Thus, filled with trust we looked for documents; we also replied impudently to all objections. The best documents would serve our case and objections, as proof.

Until now, 31 May 1905, our trust has not been betrayed.

Chapter VII

An Ecclesiastical Inquiry

Until the purchase of 14 November 1892, we had avoided as much as possible attracting attention to Panaghia, we had been careful to let others remain ignorant of our real plans concerning the precious sanctuary. Thus, we had enjoyed, it can be said, a certain privacy. Meanwhile, because of our frequent journeys to the mountain, the fact began to be known by people; some curiosity was aroused.

On 29 November 1892, I went to meet His Exc. Monsignor Timoni to fix the hour of his celebration in our College. I thought the time had come to inform him of our discovery. This was not an act of temerity, not after all the authentification established by us during those last sixteen months. After all, was it right that the Archbishop of the Diocese should be one of the last to be informed?

Thus, I recounted to his Excellency how we had been led to look, what we had found; we were sure we had discovered the House described by the Visionary of Dülmen, probably the Holy Virgin's House.

Monsignor Timoni listened to me very religiously and with pleasure.

"Oh! How happy I am!" he exclaimed." I always thought and said, that not only did the Holy Virgin come to Efesus but she died in St. John's arms!!"

I said some more about Panaghia, after which I added thoughtlessly: "We are thinking of making use of our holiday and going up there tomorrow".

"I will come with you" said the Prelate quickly. God knows if I had thought or been prepared for that! I was embarrassed because it was difficult in those days to take an Archbishop to such a place.

How would I get him up there? Where could we receive him? I tried sincerely to make him change his mind. "But Reverend! Your Grace! You cannot! It is the day of your feast!" "Yes, yes I can." "But Your Excellency, you will have visitors:" "No, I will arrange to be free'."

How I regretted my imprudence: I was looking for expedients, when a sudden volt-face came to my mind: "Well, Your Excellency, you will come: But you will come as Archbishop, Diocesan Chief, for an official inquiry." "Accepted." "Do please choose commissaries to come and testify with you." "Perfect. I will choose and name commissaries".

When I got to Sacré-Cour with this absolutely unexpected news, general applause broke out. We all were feeling in ourselves, that our discoveries were as conscious and perfectly established as could be. Nothing was lacking but to give them an official consecration, also the authentic seal of truth. Providence was there, anticipating our wishes; the Principal of the Diocese himself offered to be the witness for the public and the Church. Could we wish for more?

In order to let Monsignor prepare his journey, the date was been fixed for 1st December. Meanwhile we had been up there since Wednesday: M. Jung, Borrel, Binson, Andreas, Pélécas and Constantin Grollot to clean the place, take photographs, prepare the provisions and horses.

Thursday 1st of December 1892, 7.30 in the morning saw the departure for Ayasoulouk. The Clergy was composed of His Exc. Monsignor Andre Timoni, Archbishop of Smyrna, Apostolic Vicar of Asia Minor, Papal Delegate, Principal of the Commission; Dom Marc Varthaliti, Chancellor of the Diocese, Reverend Hambar, Canon of the Basilica of St. John, Octave Mirzan, priest of the the Basilica of St. John, M. Poulin, Superior of the Lazarists, M. Vasseur, Procuror of the

Lazarists. Laics: M. de Coursan: Director of Régie, M. Giuseppe Maroni, Chapel Master, M. François Missir of Frayssinet, all of whom were to join the Commission as well as Doctor Repin; but at the last moment these gentlemen were impeded.

The Commission was composed of twelve members, including those who went up the day before, seven ecclesiastics: His Excellency Monsignor and five laics who were joined by Pélécas, C. Grollot, Andrea, Moustapha and the horsemen.

M. Binson waited for us at Ayasoulouk. We had taken care to prepare a special horse for Monsignor, with a violet caparison bearing, His Excellency's initials, the bridle adorned with tassels. We wished to honour our Archbishop in the presence of the Turks and the Greek schismatists.

It was past 9.30 when the cavalcade left the railway-station. I was near Monsignor, and as we were going on I made a remark to His Excellency about some of the details referred to by C. Emmerich.

Having arrived at the mountain, we left the road to ride leftwards along the paved way. "Your Excellency, what is this road?"

"Oh I know it. I have been here before; it is the old road to Aidin."

"So, the old Roman road which led to Tralles, and from Tralles to Apamee, from Apamee to Antioch through the cols of the Taurus, mountains and from there joined the road to Jerusalem."

A little farther on: "Monsignor which direction are we going in?"

"Southwards. Being noon we have the sun before us."

Then, "Excellence, do you see this mountain ? Which side is it? According to our position? "On our right" "Very well; so it will be on the left for somebody coming from Jerusalem."

"Obviously". "From which side of the mountain would one reach Efesus?"

"It looks steep and inaccessible". "Perfect, Excellency. Read please; "Upon a mountain on the left when coming from Jerusalem. This mountain is a peak on the Efesus side. "We were at the place where mountain path is. "Excellency, where are we in relation to Efesus?" "On the South side, Efesus is behind us." "Please, Excellency, read." On the South one meets paths, leading to a desolate mountain." "On which side do we leave Efesus, on the right or on the left?" "On our right" "So that is West. That means we are at the same time South and East of Efesus. Please read, Excellency:" "Coming from the South-east, one sees the city huddled at the bottom of a mountain."

At eleven o'clock we arrived at the boundaries of the property. As we had to return the same evening by the 4 o'clock train, it was important to save time. We left the steps and went straight through Bulbul-dagh; from Bulbul-Dagh to the terrace, the Castle and the House.

M. Binson, who was a good rider, went ahead during our ascent, galloping like a deer through the bushes. As for us novice riders, we followed as well as we could, being careful first of all to not fall off our horses. I supposed His Excellency Monsignor Timoni didn't arrive undamaged at the top of Bulbul-Dagh, because first I saw his horse, then Monsignor, coming on foot... On the hilltop at Bulbul-Dagh we established the accuracy of C. Emmerich's sayings:

1- About Efesus: On one side the sea, on the other side the peaks of Samos.

2- About Panaghia: closer to the sea than to Efesus.

3- Meandering streams flowing from the railway station across the plain, zigzagging, reaching the foot of the mountain and seeming to separate the Christian colony settled on the terrace from the city of Prion. We only crossed the terrace; but a glance was sufficient to establish that it was situated, as the Visionary had stated, towards the top of the mountain, extending exactly as indicated; sandy spaces were seen, also the remains of old fruit-trees.

The Castle astonished all of them with its structure. With its long, large blocks seen in relief was it not a simple hut of charcoal-burners. This small hill of ruins, these two walls shelving underground, one towards the hollow, the other through the terrace up towards the peak of Bulbul Dagh... This had been an important building in ancient times, it could have been, as C. Emmerich says: "A Castle near to it, and dwelt in by a King, a friend of St. John!.."

After the Castle we reached the Chapel of Panaghia. It was late in the day. Following a small dinner on the terrace in the open air, we started to examine the House. I'll not go into the details of all that was said and done, or I would never finish; it is described fully in the Inquiry's official report, which was then re-read and approved. I will describe in general how it proceeded.

He took the vision book and read slowly. At every detail he paused, to give time to all the commissaries to see well, to judge well, to verify everything well. A point had been established and they went to another to discuss and establish it. Everything was examined like this. When I say everything",, I mean everything we had discovered and experienced ourselves in that period.

The Holy Cross Way was not included in the inquiry. Because we are not yet sure about the stations and the Cross Way itself, we did not submit the subject to the Commission.

The Virgin's Grave is not included in the official report, as it has not been found yet.

Other details are not mentioned because they are not clear.

After they had viewed everything at length, examined the whole and the details, the Commission pronounced unanimiously about the striking conformity between Panaghia and C. Emmerich's descriptions. Later, an official report was drawn up to establish officially and authentically the decisions arrived at after the visit.

This report was submitted to the commissaries in order to be signed. Everyone signed; only M. de Curson abstained, not because he was against, he assured us, but because of his position. He was dependent on the Turks and, because of his official position he was afraid that by signing the report he would offend them.

Hereafter the Official Report with the reflections, the preambles, conclusions and signatures of the Commissaries, minus M. de Curson.

MINUTES of the official visit to Panaghia Capoulou by His Excellency Monsignor Andre Timoni, Archbishop of Smyrna, Vicar Apostolic of Asia Minor;

"We, Andre Polycarpe Timoni, Archbishop of Smyrna and Vicar Apostolic of Asia Minor, also the undersigned, attest and certify the following:

"For sixteen months recently research has been done according to the indications of Sister C. Emmerich, seriously attracting country-wide attention. The place is situated near Efesus and named Panaghia Capoulou (Door of the Virgin). We wanted to verify for ourselves the veracity of the reports given to us. For this reason, on Thursday, December 1st 1892, we went to the place called Panaghia Capoulou. There we found ruins, well preserved, of an ancient house or chapel, whose construction, as the sayings of competent archaeologists state, could be 1st century A.D., The position and interior plan of this looks entirely like C. Emmerich's Revelations of the Holy Virgin's House at Efesus.

The Visionary says: "About three and half leagues from Efesus, on the Left side of the road coming from Jerusalem, - on a mountain, where from one side is seen Efesus and the sea on the other side... It is nearer to the sea, than to Efesus...." (The Holy Virgin's Life, by Catherine Emmerich, 6th edition, Castermann, 1878, pages 461,462,474).

All these details are exact.

It took three hours to get up to the house, and two hours to get down. It is exactly on the left side of the road coming from Jerusalem,-it is up on a mountain, it is reached by narrow paths from the South of Efesus. When one gets to the mountain, from the mountain-top one sees effectively on one side Efesus and on the other side, the sea, which is nearer than Efesus.

The Visionary says: "Behind, at a short distance; there are high rocks and in the neighbourhood there was a castle dwelt in by an unthroned King, a friend of St. John.... On the mountain top there was a high terrace, well-planted." (Pages 463-462)

Twelve metres behind the house are high, vertical rocks, 40-50 meters in height. At a distance of 15-20 metres there are ruins, huge blocks of an old rectangular building, supposed to be the Castle. The terrace has always been there, today it is a tobacco field.

The Visionary speaks finally of a small wood, not far from the house.... a stream, strongly meandering, through and between the mountain and Efesus. (Pages 462-463)

At ten minutes' distance from the house, there is a small valley full of small trees; a little further down and to the left a bosquet. Could this be the remains of a small wood?

The stream has disappeared; certainly it existed, as can be seen.

1) Five or six streams still furrow the plain as C. Emmerich described.

2) Other authors, particularly M.G. Weber, who speaks about it after Strabo says that two streams flow together, Marnas and Selinus.

II. - About the house,

C. Emmerich says: "The house is stone-built, there are two rooms, one at the front, one at the back." (pages 462-463)

The house is really stone-built, and it is of the same construction as the Gymnasium at Efesus.

The two rooms exist; one at the front, one at the back, one behind the other. These two rooms today are preceded by a Vestibule made in the same century but added later, annexed to the principal construction side by side.

She says: "the house ended in a platform (flat roof?) the second room's ceiling is shaped like a vault."

"The platformed (flat)roof has completely disappeared, also that of the second room; but on both side walls a vault is visible.

She says: "The back room ended in a niche and the back of that room was the oratory of the Holy Virgin." (pg. 463)

The back of this room ends in a niche in the form of a round prominence on the outside. It would be possible to place an altar in the inside part.

She says: "The windows were high, the second room was darker than the first." (pg. 462-463)

The Windows are 2,50m. from the ground. The back room was darker than the first; easy to understand- this room received light only from the back end through a very narrow window 3m. from the ground.

She says: "The second room is separated from the first by a hearth between two doors, one on each side." (pg. 462-463)

The hearth and doors disappeared when the Apostles transformed the modest house into a chapel (C. Emmerich's report pg.507). The two prominences on the right and left in the wall between the two rooms still show clearly today where the hearth and doors were.

She says: "On the right side of the oratory, leaning upon a niche formed in the wall was the Virgin's bedroom. On the front left side of the oratory was another room for linen and furniture." (pg. 465)

"The doors leading to the oratory and rooms," says C. Emmerich, "are actually walled up but still visible." Nothing can be said for the moment about the room on the left side where linen was kept.

"The Virgin's room is in ruins, but open: one can see the niche on which the room was supported at the rear where the bed stood, the oratory being near the bedstead." (pg.492)

She says: "The Virgin's couch was against the wall, one foot high and half the ordinary length and width."

At the back of the room, a projection 0.45 cm from the ground had been put there with the purpose of supporting the Virgin's couch.

She says finally that a curtain from one end of the room to the other closed off the oratory placed between them. This is evident from a simple inspection of the Place.

Conclusion

On the one hand: the respect given to Catherine Emmerich by her superiors and her contemporaries, proving her virtue and faith, mean that her Revelations merit at least some trust.

On the other: verifying with the book and seeing the perfect conformity which exists for the place as well as the house in ruins which we have visited, all that the Visionary says about the Holy Virgin's House is true.

Knowing also the local traditions, having referred to the subject recently and especially, these confirm that the Holy Virgin dwelt in three different places near Efesus, lastly at Panaghia-Capolou, where she died and where her grave should be.

We believe the ruins of Panaghia Capoulou are really the remains of the house where the Holy Virgin lived and we beseech the Good Mother to help us to bring light to this question which concerns the Church of Smyrna first and also Catholics all over the world.

A.P.Timoni
Arch. of Smyrna, vic. ap.

Varthaliti, canon
Chancellor of archbishopric

D. Eugene Hambar
Canon of the Basilica of St. John

Jules Borrel
Director of the French Post Office at Smyrna

Abbé Octave Mirzan
Priest of the Basilica of St.John

Evangelist
Giuseppe Moroni

Chapel Master
J. Vasseur
p.d.l.m.

H.Jung p.d.l.m.
Professor of Science

E. Poulin
Superior of the College of Propaganda at Smyrna

G. Binson
Depositor of the Ottoman
Regie of Tobacco at Smyrna.

Paul d'Andria
Engineer

Minutes taken by: Gaspard Dumont
p.d.l.m. Minutes Clerk

On 14th January 1893, Dom Marco Varthaliti, in the name of the Archbishopric, officially gave me the document approved, accepted and properly signed.

This document is precious, very precious for the Panaghia Capoulou case. Before it was only our private witness, of private value; today we can show urbi and orbi an authentic witness, an official and irrefutable authenticity.

Let us add that there is another precious advantage: we are not alone any more in maintaining the case for Panaghia. With us and after us there are convinced friends, as many ecclesiastics as laics, and most of all His Excellency Andre Timoni, Archbishop of Smyrna.

Chapter VIII

Panaghia and Public Opinion

How did Smyrna accept Panaghia ? How did Christians accept Panaghia?

There are the two points we will expound to you in this chapter.

I. Panaghia and Smyrna

The official inquiry of his Excellency Monsignor Timoni on 1st December 1892 came as a shock which brought Panaghia Capoulou's history to the notice of the city. Since that moment, everyone has been talking about it.

The Jews, having no interest, remained indifferent. The Gregorians did the same, so did the Turks, more strangers to us than the others. However, seriously, who gave us the first favourable witness about Panaghia-Capouli? It was the Turks. We have related elsewhere Mary's grave, on Page 7-8, the fact of the Cavasse of the French Post Office, Mehmet, who in 1890, long before the Discovery, found on the ground a medal of the Holy Virgin and pretended to recognise the image of the Great Lady who had died at Efesus. We spoke with the same cavasse today at the French Hospital; he served for a while as a gendarme in the Efesus area, and he, too, had observed the same tradition as referred to above.

While all these people, Jews, Gregorians and Turks remained outside of the Discovery, it was different for Greeks and Catholics.

The Greeks launched a campaign "for Panaghia". There is a trace of this first impression in "Amalthia" of 8-20 April 1896. We will relate it later in the article "Polemics." I had even heard at that time about a list of subscriptions made in order to gather the necessary funds to buy the ancient sanctuary, hung up on the door of Aghia Photini. But our divided Brothers soon knew the Latins were in possession of the precious relic.

Immediately, there was a sudden and complete volte-face. It was evident that the Orthodox had in the past respected Panaghia-Capoulou. Amalphia testifies (See note). But enough of the past!.. Since the moment when Panaghia escaped from the Greeks to belong to the Catholics, it was no longer a sacred place for them to venerate. The Virgin had not died up there; there were only vulgar ruins, just like many others; worthless, without any merit in the eyes of Holy Orthodoxy.

The Greek Church replied with these good feelings and since then has maintained a deep silence. There was no interest in Panaghia, it was as if she had never existed... until 1896. I verified with astonishment that Panaghia was going quietly on her way and my spirits rose when the Orthodox church felt the need to abandon her majestic silence, "to take in hand the hammer of truth" and "the heavy axe of history", in order to strike at the head of this terrible lie, this inconsistent and falsified hypothesis... and all the bastard publications.. "whereby that execrable "Papist Church" was attempting "to mislead" the wonderfully good Orthodox Church, because of "C. Emmerich's dreams, also the pretended discovery of Panaghia Capoulou."

Catholics accepted Panaghia more frankly. Had they all been of the same idea, the same feelings? Oh no!! This meant to be ignorant of the poor human heart with the petty passions which agitate it, to suppose for one instant a perfect, absolute accord. Our Lord is God; He preaches the Gospel to the crowds, his predications are followed by numerous healings, miracles. 2000 years later, how many still refuse to believe in the Gospel! We would like to think that Panaghia has bound all convictions together Things do not happen like this in life; Panaghia has the destiny of all great causes; there have been partisans, there have been adversaries, and between them the floating troop of abstainers or prudent types who always wait to pronounce later.

The known adversaries have been almost exclusively among the Clergy. The Reverend P. Bernard, Superior of the Dominicans and Punta, Sainte Marie and Recollets, Monsignor Cannavo and most of the Capuchins, some priests and laics, a very small number; all those who had not seen and who refused to go to see. No-one from the Dames de Sion had gone to Panaghia, either. (1910)

I said "adversaries." Oh, adversaries well mitigated, no dangerous fighting between them! They never attack frankly, they attack without any serious argument to certify their convictions or their prejudice. However, they must not forget that the Diocesan Authority has pronounced officially and very categorically and in full knowledge of the matter. It would be disrespectful to argue without having seen the place or studied the question seriously.

Most of the clergymen and even more the faithful people followed their Archbishop with enthusiasm. There were some privileged families who had seen for themselves. These first believers "made the snow melt" so well that the majority of our Catholics are now for Panaghia.

In Smyrna devotion is expansive and spreads quickly. Could it have been devotion or curiosity that was speaking about a pilgrimage to Panaghia? This is the moment to remember a previous fact, ten years old, which is closely related to our subject.

In May, 1884 the good parish priest of Budja, maybe to please the Sisters, maybe to give a lift to his May month prayers, transferred the pious exercises to the Sisters' new chapel. He proposed to a Capuchin friar of Budja, that the Reverend Jean-Baptiste, a new French priest, come to preach every day's instruction. He accepted with pleasure. He was appreciated. He conceived the thought of organising a pilgrimage to Efesus, of glorifying Mary in the same place where she had been named by the universal church, officially proclaimed Mother of God.

The proposition of the pilgrimage was not well received. They exclaimed, "Chimera! Extravagance!" joking quite sharply. The Reverend went to the Archbishop, who approved at once. "I will lead it!". It had been decided.

28th of May. The pilgrimage was announced in all the parishes. There was a complete change of mood!!

28th May. Since 5 o'clock in the morning the railway station had been overflowing, although the train's departure was 2 hours later. Forty-four wagons were hardly sufficient to transport all the pilgrims. What a crowd! What enthusiasm, also what piety! On top of the first waggon fluttered the French flag; every wagon was adorned with flags; from all the doors came the sound of canticles, hymns and prayers.

At departure time, a telegram was sent to the Sovereign Pontiff to inform him of the first pilgrimage to Efesus, asking his Holiness to bless the pilgrims.

As soon as it arrived at Ayasoulouk, the procession was organised. The Holy Virgin's flag at its head was carried by the priest of the Cathedral, Dom Pavlo Issaverdens, then came the Sisters with the young people followed by hundreds of pilgrims. Thus, they moved slowly towards the Mosque of Selim, where the remains of the ancient Basilica of St. John were. Prayers were said aloud, reciting the Rosary. This took three quarters of an hour. Never had Ayasoulouk appeared so imposing, so edifying a spectacle. All Catholic Smyrna was present, from the city and the suburbs; the secular clergy were all there, religious communities, families in large numbers, hundreds and hundreds of pilgrims. On the Mosque's threshold, the head of the procession started the Litanies to give time for the rest of the pilgrims to arrive. They gathered around the makeshift altar (made for the occasion) and above the altar the French flag waved.

They were at the end of the litanies when, from far away, a melody was heard; it was a group from Aidin arriving in procession, with a flag preceding a long cortége of Sisters and young girls.

At ten o'clock the Mass started in perfect silence. Around his Excellency, numerous clergy, many heterodox priests, attracted by the novelty of the spectacle, and edified by what they saw. "Ah, these Catholics," they said to each other. "How beautifully they pray." "They have the real religion, we are only poor and blind".

Voices, hymns for the occasion rang out throughout the Mass. At the moment of the Holy Communion, forty persons were present before the Holy Table. Everybody was deeply moved, everybody's soul was delighted by this most pious experience.

After the mass, His Excellency read a consecration to the Holy Virgin and expressed to the pilgrims the great joy he felt. He saw in this mass of pilgrims plenty of graces for his dear Diocese. Later, his soul oveflowing, he declared his belief in the stay and death of the Holy Virgin at Efesus. He called at the numerous churches of Ionio dedicated to the Dormition of the Holy Virgin. He remembered particularly a local tradition he had witnessed himself! He was, as he said, on a pastoral visit to give the Sacrament of Confirmation to the small number of Catholics who lived around Smyrna. He had arrived at a place called Metelin or Ayvali. They invited him to visit the ruins of an ancient church. He accepted: the first thing that attracted his attention was an old repainting presenting the Virgin's death.

"What is this?" I asked the country folk. "This, Monsignor, is the Virgin, who died in this country". And the Prelate demanded, "Where does it come from if it is not a tradition? Everything makes us believe it. C. Emmerich is right when she assures us that the Holy Virgin died at Efesus and that her Grave is there. The Visionary says that one day they will find the grave, then there will be great joy all over the world, especially in the Orient.

"Let us be holily proud, my brothers," concluded his Excellency. "to possess such a precious relic; let us pray to Mary with trust, great trust, that this beautiful church of Efesus will be restored as it was in olden times, to bless us."

The peroration ended thus. His Excellency blessed the pilgrims. Everybody went to the tables disposed around the mosque, opened their baskets of provisions and lunched with joy.

Groups of Turks sat farther away, looking curiously at this joyful spectacle. When the dinner ended, His Excellency went among the tables to collect the remains and meanwhile the crowd of pilgrims spread out over the meadows to visit the ruins Meanwhile, the good Pastor distributed to poor Turks the provisions he had collected. It had been a feast for these poor people. How they blessed the charitable Pastor and the charitable Catholics...

Late in the evening they gathered again before the mosque for a last prayer; later, they went to the rail-station in procession, saying litanies. Everyone took his seat in a waggon and the train moved away. Then the Magnificat, a last call of love towards this good Mother, was sung. It was also an expression of thanks for the good day they had spent at Efesus.

If I have taken a long time to report this first pilgrimage to Efesus, it is because it was the precursor of Panaghia. The mysterious affinities between this first pilgrimage to Efesus and the pilgrimage which would follow, will be described later. But let us come to our subject. Two things remained from the Efesus pilgrimage:

1) a deep memory of pure joy of this beautiful day,

2) the decision to renew, every five years, the same pilgrimage.

May, 1884 saw the first pilgrimage, May, 1889 the second. The third would take place in May 1894. The time was approaching.. Smyrna's Catholics had claimed their pilgrimage. Now it will be better understood what the thought of Panaghia added to their ardour and their wishes.

Before arranging anything, His Excellency Monsignor Timoni himself came to Sacré-coeur on Sunday, 29th April, 1894 to speak about the subject "They are pressing me," said he, "About the pilgrimage; but firstly I wish to know if you see it as an inconvenience or an advantage." We were not ready for such a question. We asked His Excellency for time to think about it.

Next day, the 30th, we gathered for a Council. M. Binson was asked to give his ideas, and he made many very judicious observations. The 'teskere' for the house had been promised, but not yet delivered. If there was going to be a pilgrimage, they maybe would find some stupid pretext to stop the construction. It was important not to arouse any suspicion, either in the Turks or in the Greeks. There was nothing more likely to excite hostility than a public and popular manifestation, such as an official pilgrimage to Panaghia. "Look at these Franks", the Greeks will yell. "As soon as they bought the sanctuary, they were in a hurry to hold great ceremonies!!". The Turks would say, "What impudence to hold a ceremony like that in our country, right under our noses, as if they were in their own country, this is a provocation!!"

If you restrict the pilgrimage to Efesus, as in the past, you will not be able to stop the curious or the audacious from disobeying, ignoring your restriction and going to Panaghia in spite of everything!! On the other hand, you risk setting the multitude against Panaghia. They will not understand your reasons for prudence.

"Why are they forbidding us? That is because there is nothing up there!". When the house is built, there will be no reason to be afraid of Turks or Greeks, we will be on our own land. Then the pilgrimages will take place; one, two to Panaghia as in 84-

89, a second only for the most ardent. Then we can say to the Turks: "Do you see, it is just like the past." For the time being a pilgrimage is not possible, not before the completion of the construction work. Later it could be two pilgrimages at the same time: if the pilgrimage to Panaghia is a success, that will be good! If not, there is no need to dwell on it, because the official pilgrimage would be the one to Efesus.

The Council discussed these reasons and referred later to His Excellency the Archbishop. The pilgrimage was postponed until September or October the same year, or to May the following year.

September and October passed, nobody mentioned the pilgrimage. We were careful not to remind them.

In early spring, 1895, these was no word about the pilgrimage. We thought they had forgotten. We were inwardly thanking God, when on Friday 24th of May, His Excellency Monsignor spoke again about the pilgrimage. "Oh Monsignor, the season is over. Is it possible to get up to Panaghia in this heat? You will get sunstroke! Or a fever! Late April would be the right moment, today it would be a disaster; a disaster for us, a disaster for Panaghia if any accidents happened." The observation was appropriate. Monsignor understood it well. "What can be done?" he said, disappointed. "Your Excellency could postpone it to a better season, for example, next Autumn." We agreed to next Autumn in the hope that it would be postponed again, and it has been.

We had succeeded in postponing the pilgrimage project. It can be understood how little we wanted it, even more, how afraid we were of trouble. If, at least, the pilgrimage had been organised and regularised, if it had been His Excellency Timoni's, the Clergy's, and the community's task, not ours, as it has been until today.

1896: We had to aquiesce, the pressure had become irresistible.

On 12th May the Archbishop summoned the Council at the Archbishop's residence to arrange the details of the pilgrimage.

1) There would be two pilgrimages: one to Efesus, at the Mosque of Selim as before, presided over by His Excellency Monsignor Connova, the second to Panaghia, under the presidency of His Excellency Monsignor Timoni.

2) Day: Wednesday, 20th May, 5 o'clock in the morning.

3) The pilgrimage would be announced and notices posted up in all the parishes.

4) A committee of pious laics would be charged with making arrangements with the railway and the procedures of the local authorities, regarding the responsibility for the pilgrimage.

5) Everyone would take his own provisions for the day. It was, for the Catholics, universal emotion. Everyone had his reasons for going: the pious and the curious would be satisfied to see Panaghia; the indifferent and opponents would remain at Efesus.

M. Binson and Borrel went ahead to prepare horses, and negotiate with the local police. M. Jung and Vasseur went up to Panaghia on the eve of the pilgrimage with Brother Kolly and his cook, Nicolas, to prepare the dinner. It was the first pilgrimage to Panaghia; they lacked experience, but it might be successful. They were greatly preoccupied this time, but the next would be better.

That day, all the city was in commotion. At our College we woke at 3 o'clock, attended mass at 3.30. At 4 o'clock, there was breakfast for the students; 4,30 saw the departure of the trumpet flourish under the direction of M.M. Aluta, Veron. Monsignor left a little later.

At five o'clock precisely, all the people were assembled at the railway station, 1172 full tickets included half places for 1300/1400 persons. The last pilgrimage in 1889 had consisted of 700 persons. Two trains were needed to transport all the people: one train of 30 waggons, a second of 20.

I have not described people's feelings, but their pious prayers during the journey were full of enthusiasm. After arriving at 7 o'clock at Ayasoulouk, the pilgrims separated into groups.

One group, among them the Capuchin friars, the Franciscans, Italians, Dame de Sion and their pupils made their way towards the Selim Mosque with His Excellency Monsignor Cannavo. The rest, the majority, took the path towards the mountain, to Panaghia.

During the departure for Panaghia there had been a moment of confusion. Having considered the length and difficulty of the journey, as a precaution we had got horses, donkeys and mules ready for the weak or tired. Among these animals we reserved a dozen horses for his Excellency Monsignor and his suite; also thirty donkeys for the children of the trumpet flourish.

But in spite of putting aside the reserved animals, they left them by themselves, they escaped from the others, as there was nobody there to guard them. When the people got the train, the crowd hurried up to the donkeys and horses, everyone taking what he found. Meanwhile, M. Binson was looking for Monsignor, M. Vasseur was running after his group; There was nobody to deal with the animals. When we arrived, we found our animals being ridden by others. A little more confusion, and the "Episcopal suite" would end up by walking! Thank God! Everything was arranged, and continued in perfect order until the end.

In the middle of the plain someone stopped the pilgrims, also his Excellency and his suite. It was M. Rubellin, the photographer who wished to take pictures of Monsignor and the pilgrims. We started out again cheerfully; all of sudden, drops of moisture fell between the Gymnasium and the mountain; soon the drops changed to rain as we were passing through the valley which leads to the mountain road. M. Larigaldie saved the situation. "Ahead", he shouted and rushed towards the mountain. They opened umbrellas and followed him. The rain stopped, having freshened the atmosphere to the great advantage of the pedestrians, who were suffering from the heat.

It was a graceful and picturesque sight, this crowd zigzagging up the mountain, some walking, some on donkeys, some on horses: here there were groups, there isolated pilgrims, who rushed ahead intrepidly to arrive earlier, in spite of their sweat. The crowd of pilgrims made their way up slowly, stopping at intervals to rest, also to admire the delightful and impressive view.

M. Jung had thought of it all, for placed along the road at intervals there was a child to offer the thirsty a glass of fresh water.

At 8.30, the first pilgrims had started to emerge on the mountain. Monsignor had dismounted from his horse to finish the journey on foot and he was one of the last to arrive.

On arrival, he took his crosier and mitre and, accompanied by the Clergy, he advanced towards the Chapel, which was adorned for the occasion with different flowers, sprigs of greenery and branches. Flags adorned the facade, others spread like veils, forming a tent above the altar. In front of the door a triumphal arcade with sylvan ornaments. The crowd filled the sanctuary, and, pressed agaist the doors, surged out onto the esplanade, silent and pious. Up on the high mast waved the French flag.

His Excellency Monsignor announced plenary indulgence accorded "by heart" to the pilgrims of Panaghia and Efesus. Soon after the mass in the chapel began, attended by Missions Superior and many priests. Outside, the trumpet flourishes alternating between hymns, musical pieces accompanied slowly by the brass. During the offertory there a fresh alert; the rain had started again. The water was dripping through the flags over our heads, falling on the altar, on the corporal, in the chalice, on us. Fortunately, it was a small shower sufficient to put the flourish off, and condemned it to silence for the rest of the day.

Very beautiful, very beautiful was the pious attitude of the pilgrims, the ardour of their prayers! We had counted about twenty/thirty communions, as a precaution we had prepared 150 hosts in the ciborium.

After the 49th we perceived we did not have enough hosts.

They were cut in two, which provided a hundred and four communions. Most of these pious souls had got up early in the morning, walked, remained with an empty stomach until ten o'clock to have the high honour of taking communion at Mary's House, where Mary had prayed so many times. An old lady, half dead with tiredness, almost losing consciousness, refused to eat anything. "No, no!" she said she also wanted to take holy communion in the Holy Virgin's House. Poor woman! They had to hold her under the arms to take her to the altar. She had been counselled. May our Lord bless her for her generosity.

A Magnificat roared out from 700 chests. Thus the morning ceremony finished religiously. His Excellency Monsignor, who led the procession to the House, stopped again half-way for photographs. Finally Monsignor left the house; everybody dispersed on the mountain or in the valley looking for a place picnic. The Clergy lunched with us, so did the committee, guests were numerous.

Rain fell again, but the afternoon was bright. The devout, or rather the devout women took advantage of this to recite the Rosary. M. Larigaldie in a surplice led them in their singing and prayer. Most of the pilgrims went down to the ruins for an early dinner. Later they made their way en masse to the railway station for departure. At 5 o'clock, the first train being full of people, the second was to be for His Excellency, his suite and the rest of the pilgrims. On the way back to Smyrna everyone felt a sweet desire to visit Panaghia again. During the day, a number of little miracles took place.

I will relate only two: Miss Marie Fidano, who cannot stay with an empty stomach, waited from 4 o'clock the morning until eleven to take the Communion without any trouble.

M. Velay, an asthmatic, who could not walk from his house to his business, from the Rue Moscow until the quay, without being out of breath, walked all the way to Panaghia, going and returning in good condition. "Look at me", he was saying, "I am not tired."

There is something else I should like to relate. Why did nobody make a profit? Carpouza of Ayasoulouk knew about the pilgrimage. He had hurried to prepare a quantity of food, for he was counting on good business. But nobody went... Andreas for his own part had set up a small shop with cakes drinks, zinzibirs and other refreshments. He didn't sell anything, either. The Holy Virgin didn't want any idea of making money, even honestly, during this pious pilgrimage.

It would be like this in the future, during pilgrimages; no small dinners prepared down there, nor sellers of water on the way, nor coffee and zinzibirs up there. It would also be prohibited to collect money during the pilgrimage.

The pilgrimage of 20th May had left a good impression. Some wished to go up again. Since Easter 1897, people had been speaking of such a pilgrimage. Actually, an annual pilgrimage to Panaghia could take place. However, we wished to be relieved of any responsibility, once and for all, now and for the future. It was important to make clear at the start, frankly and clearly, the true characteristics of the pilgrimage. We wished absolutely to make it known. It is the pilgrimage of Smyrna and the Diocese, not of the Lazarists. This was in order to put a stop to jokes, jealousy and let everybody know the importance of the pilgrimage.

For this reason, we closed our ears to all advances, solicitations and pressures. "Do you wish to go on the pilgrimage? Good! Make an arrangement with His Excellency the Monsignor! Don't expect anything from us".

In the face of this decision from our side, they retreated. There wasn't any pilgrimage that year. But our Catholics didn't accept defeat. In '98 they came back again, but this time they knew how to proceed.

They had understood our decision; they agreed among themselves. They were looking for the necessary authorisation and procedure. Withal was at the head of the movement. Monsignor designated Dom Michele from Budja as spiritual adviser; finally the day was decided; Sunday 22nd May, 1898. None of us interfered, nor did we appear during the negotiations, nor for the pilgrimage itself.

This second pilgrimage was not so bright as the first, but it was also successful; 500-600 pilgrims participated. It had the advantage of informing Catholics how they should proceed for future pilgrimages, and this was an excellent result. No committee, more a hindrance than a help, no long speeches or preparations. Some days before Easter they came to see us: "Would you mind if there was a pilgrimage?" "No, not at all!" They went to Monsignor, they agreed on the day, the persons responsible, the publicity, etc. The day of the pilgrimage, the persons responsible walking ahead, they set out with God's Grace.

It is simple, as one can see. Already they know. We are actually in our 9th pilgrimage now. They were all accomplished piously, in perfect order and to everybody's satisfaction.

We said that M. Withall had been the person responsible for the second pilgrimage. M. Borrel dealt with the third, with MM.Ch. Fidao, Ch. Salzani, Ernest Pagy, Guys and Giustiniani and Monsignor, who himself organised the fourth on 3rd April,

1902. Cros Etienne and Mirzan Andre the fifth, on Sunday 27th April the same year.

Since then it has been M. Cros, almost alone, who has done the organising, making contact with the Archbishop, the railway, etc. etc. He does it without any fuss, any embarrassment, and it is well done.

The first pilgrimage had been in May. This was difficult for the school classes and late for the season. Since the third pilgrimage, they decided it would be better for all on the Wednesday of Easter. The students were on holiday, the teachers free, the Clergy free also. Everybody was joyfully looking forward to the Easter Feast. The chosen day was a success. We saw a lot of students, religious brothers and sisters of different orders, etc. etc.

Some insisted on Monday, M. Jung was for either. "No!" we said to them. "You risk meeting tourists for whom the pilgrimage is a pleasant party, maybe they will disturb the mass, being on the ruins or elsewhere."

Experience proved this fact. In May, 1904, after the pilgrimage of Easter Wednesday, which was successful, the Reverend Jean-Baptiste, Superior of St. Polycarp, whose initiative and animation are known; decided to organise a second pilgrimage to Panaghia, this time, on the Sunday.. "Go, go, friends: the roads are open!!...."

He made great preparations, posted up notices, he gave a lot of publicity to "the Great Pilgrimage" and he rushed around.... Finally Sunday 8th May, the day of the pilgrimage arrived.

It was at the railway station that the first disappointment was suffered. In spite of all the publicity, noise, and promised "attractions", only 450 persons came, in spite of the 1500-2000 announced.

To attract more people and to satisfy them, he promised two pilgrimages; one to Efesus at the church of the Council, with mass hymns, predication, vespers, Angelus etc. etc. The second to Panaghia with trumpet flourishes. The Good Reverend Jean-Baptiste counted on the good will of his people, also on the ability of his organisation. What had happened? As soon as they got off from the train, the trumpeters of the flourish escaped on the way to the ruins, trumpets in mouth, a lot of pilgrims following after. The Rev. Jean-Baptiste tried to gather them, again; he called, he shouted, he advised, but in vain! At least he gave up and, followed by some devoted souls, took the mountain path. Only 72 pilgrims. The Poor Reverend, he was so disappointed. After the mass he retired, without any word of piety even to the little group of good people who had followed him and had proved their good will. M. Jung felt so ridiculous, he didn't appear all day long. That was the journey there.

The journey back was worse. The pilgrims were suffering from thirst, heat and annoyance. Without water, because as before, for M. Jung was not there to provide water and bring some pails.... Where could they find shelter, on this plain devoured by the sun?

What could they do from 7 o'clock in the morning until 7 p.m?. It was a disaster! Up there the pilgrims had almost no distractions. They could walk up and down, nothing more. But what of those on the way down? All of them swore they wouldn't come again. Rev. Jean-Baptiste did the same. Now it is almost sure there will not be a pilgrimage on the Sunday, even less, two!

The pilgrimages are a tradition today. There is one every year. These pilgrimages have made the whole Community of Smyrna know and love Panaghia.

When I say that, I do not mean only the Catholic community, but those of many heterodoxies; Greeks, Armenians and Protestants like to visit Panaghia and remember it well.

The Virgin rewarded the faith of many people with healings qualified as miracles and also particular graces. All this maintains and fosters devotion to Panaghia. Thus, opposition melted like snow under the sun.

I will not pretend there is not still some of the old opposition, but that lasted only until 1895. This year, 1895, has been a providential year:

For many months Sister Grancey had been pressing me to inform the Holy Father, who had other things to do than to occupy himself with our discovery. Let the good Lord do that! He knows when to inform the Pope! Without us, when the moment comes. The good Sister came to me over and over on this errand. I always gave the same answer.

Or it happened thus: M. Lobry wrote me from Constantinople to inform me that an Extraordinary Commissary would be sent, to the Orient, charged by Leon XIII personally, to study the famous question of Oriental Rites in the actual place. "you pay attention, too," added the friendly M. Lobry, "Don't speak too badly of the Rites:" Who is this Extraordinary Commissary? Nobody had told me about him before. Some days later, I read in the "Univers:" Reverend P. Enschbach, order of St. Esprit, Superior of the French Seminary of Sainte Claire in Rome." "Enchbach! A name to remember", I said to myself.

One month, two, three months passed. On Saturday, 18th March, 1895, at 7 o'clock I was in Smyrna, preparing for Holy Mass, when I was called to the parlour to receive a stranger. I was in the presence of a priest in late middle age, serious and dignified of face, wearing his shoulder belt. I remarked that he wore the Roman collar.

He asked me politely if he could celebrate the mass. "Reverend, when you wish:" "I should be happy if you could give me hospitality, so that I can be near the Church."

"At your service, Reverend. We have just two free rooms at this moment". He thanked me politely. "Besides I am no stranger to the Lazarists!" Saying that, he took out from his portfolio a visiting-card which he held out to me. It was from Rome, from our Solicitor at the Holy See. He recommended him warmly.... Rev. Escbach, holder of the card. –"The enemy", I thought, but I restrained myself, and received him well.

After mass and breakfast, I was at his disposal. From 8 to 12 we visited together all the buildings. In the Community's hall, he looked at the views of Panaghia. "They told me about it, in Palestine," he said then. "I should be greatly pleased to hear about it from you yourself."

I told him, very simply, about Panaghia's discovery. He seemed very interested in the question. When I ended, he said: "I should like to see it, is it possible?" "Yes, Reverend. If you can wait until Monday, M. Jung will be free to take you there." "I will."

Monday, 20th May, early in the morning, saw their departure for Panaghia. I thoroughly primed M. Jung.." You are dealing with a serious man, wise and learned. No proselitisms, no comments! Just show him things, answer his questions; let him see for himself". "Understood," he said.

Our travellers returned towards 6.30 in the evening. I was in a hurry to know about their impressions. Thus, as soon as I could catch M. Jung alone, I asked. "Well?" "The Reverend saw all, he is in ecstasy and deep in thought." After dinner I saw the Reverend himself. "Reverend, are you pleased with your day?" "Oh yes", he replied, so coldly that I hurried to change the subject.

As soon as he was free, I caught M. Jung: "Why did you say to me that the Reverend was delighted, and quite overcome? He hardly answered me when I asked him if he was pleased, he was so cold" "What I told you is true. The Reverend was so overwhelmed that he could not conceal his emotion."

M. Jung went on: "As I was going to speak him, he said, "M. Jung leave me alone. I need to be alone in silence to better perceive what I have seen." Assured by his words, the next day I came back again discreetly to the subject of Panaghia. This time the Reverend was clearer: "Reverend," he assured me with conviction, "You have found it. I saw, in Jerusalem, what they call Mary's Grave, but it is not this. At Panaghia, everything is clear; everything, right down to those ancient walls, and I know about walls, as I wear the Roman collar. Surely you have found it."

I dared then to ask the Reverend to write down his impressions, such as they were. For some time we had been collecting the personal impressions and reflections of the pilgrims, and we preserved them carefully, as impartial statements from many different people who had seen Panaghia. The Reverend accepted my request. "Very willingly," he answered." Do you wish it to be reserved or enthusiastic?" "With reserve, Reverend. We prefer to say less but be sure, instead of saying much and later denying." "Well then with reserve. I will write to you from Athens".

The same evening, Tuesday 21st May, the Reverend left for Athens, taking with him in his suitcase some views of Panaghia taken by M. Jung, a copy of the Episcopal Report of the Enquiry, a short article about Panaghia's Discovery and, in his soul, the good and imperishable memory of his visit to the Virgin's House.

As we were not yet prepared for a debate and were looking for a clear sign from Providence, we advised the Reverend Eschbach not to make a fuss about the Discovery. He could speak, but in the right place and discreetely.

We also recommended absolute discretion about names; neither Jung, nor Poulin, the Sisters or the Lazarists would be mentioned. We did not want ourselves or the Brotherhood to be a subject of discussion. It was important to keep Panaghia's work anonymous, simple Catholic Action, as we had done since the beginning, to put aside everything that could be of personal, particular, interest. Three days later, the Reverend Eschbach wrote from Athens: "I was strongly captivated by my visit to Panaghia, and the impression gets stronger the more I think about it..... I will write to you from Rome."

On his return to Rome, the Reverend Eschbach became a convinced and ardent preacher of Panaghia. He wrote to me himself. Judging his letter by the expressions he used, it was easy to see that he was still under its spell. What beautiful things were said in this letter!

After he had dealt with the usual details in a spiritual lecture to the students of the Seminary of Sainte Claire about his journey to Jerusalem, he stopped: "Young men, I have kept until the end the most interesting part; but as discretion and prudence have been recommended to me, I will ask you to do the same. Do you promise me?" - "Yes, Reverend". "Good." And he recounted at length, with piety and love all Panaghia's history. He repeated what he had heard from others, what he had seen himself, and the deep emotion he had felt when he was in the venerable sanctuary.

Some two years later, the Reverend de Revel, one of his listeners, came to Smyrna for his brother's wedding. The Commandant de Revel was to marry Miss Salzani, the Reverend Eschbach's letter confirmed. He had promised to keep secret, at least until further orders, the matter of Panaghia. Hundreds of partisans were engaged then in Panaghia's cause, prepared to serve soon as witnesses in universo mundo.

The Rev. Eschbach didn't stop there. He visited the Pope; he gave a report about his mission in the Orient. Then he went on; "Holy Father, I bring to your Holiness a present from these countries. A beautiful, very beautiful present. He described to the Pontiff all that he had seen at Panaghia.

Leon XIII listened him with great attention and deep interest.

"Do you have photographs?" "Yes, Holy Father, here they are." The Pope looked at the photographs for a long time... and he kept them. "I have no more photographs," Rev. Eschbach wrote to me, referring to his interview with Leon XIII. "Oh Reverend, don't be sorry! Here are others to replace those the Holy Father took from you, and I thank you deeply for what you have told me! We are very happy to know that the Head of the Church found out through you about Panaghia's Discovery, and that he takes a serious interest."

This is how the Pope found out about Panaghia. We weren't involved, only Good Providence had once more disposed and arranged all things. Who was pleased? Sister Grancey.

In August 1895, M. Chevallier, our First Assistant, met Leon XIII. The Pope had spoken warmly of Panaghia, he wished even to accord indulgences. Thank you, Holy Father.

We knew later that His Holiness had taken an interest in Panaghia, following our work, our research and discoveries. As soon as I had written a letter to Reverend Eschbach, the next day a copy of an extract was on his desk. Thus he was kept informed of our progress.

The Pope's interest in Panaghia had a serious consequence. We had advised the Rev. Eschbach to be discreet about Panaghia. He, in his turn, advised his seminarists to be silent: but how could one restrict the Pope, the Cardinals, all the Roman Court. The news quickly spread to the whole of Rome! If reporters were interested, that meant the newspapers!

"La Vérité" was the first, no. 25, March, 1896, to publish Panaghia's discovery. The narrative was so exact, the description so detailed, so perfect at the same time, I suspected strongly they were bearing in mind the Official Report of Inquiry and the short note of 1893 sent from us to relatives and acquaintances.

It was known through Rome: the Reverend Eschbach, Superior of the French Seminary of Sainte Claire in Rome, then his journey to the Orient, then his pilgrimage to Panaghia... It could be said they were well informed. The Pope and Cardinals had been informed about Panaghia through him, and His Holiness was interested in Panaghia's case.

Five days later, on 30th March, La Gazette de France published in its turn a long article about the "Holy Virgin's House". It had repeated all the details given previously by La Vérité.

Two weeks after, "Le Gaulois" announced the Discovery to its readers, but it was wrong -as is all news that is very new- described as the work of Rev. Eschbach and Poulin. "L'Univers" of 25th April reported as well the notice in Le Gaulois, confirming and adding: "Soon a serious work about this important matter will be published, in order to satisfy public curiosity."

These papers, and many others, were full of news about Panaghia: "Le Bien Public" of Gand, 26th April' 96, "Le Messager de Tours," 1st August, 96. "La Semaine Réligieuse of Gand," 8th August 96. "Le Stanboul" of Constantinople, 14th October 96, then "La Poste," "Le Domino Rose," after "L'Italia," etc. etc. etc. All these newspapers were favourable to Panaghia.

By the way, Greek newspapers had also started to discuss the matter in Smyrna. "Amalthia" of 8-10 April, 96, "Amonia" of 3-15 June in Constantinople, "Neon Periodikon" (New Magazine) of mid- April, "Alithia Ecclestiastiki," the official newspaper of the Fener Patriarchate, of 4-14 June.

We had waited for a long time for the moment to speak. We had been preparing for this hour, silently, patiently. Late in 1892 the our little project was discussed and approved but when it came to its execution, a formidable obstacle opposed us from the Main House in Paris.

Since the beginning they had shown extreme scepticism about Panaghia's Discovery. In spite of inspiring more trust in centres other than the Main House, it was precisely they who were defiant, sceptical and doubting about the discovery. Others treated M. Jung's "claimed discovery" as a new trick thought up by the "farce-player" that he was. Thus, two months later, the Reverend himself wrote this letter to me:

Paris, September 1891

"Congratulating you, as well as your colleagues, for your ardour, your attachment to the Holy Virgin's worship, my Council and I beg you to continue your work on the claimed Discovery, which preoccupies so much the spirits of those around you at this moment. If could even be true, but it is not our Congregation that should deal with this matter.. Thus, I beg you to renounce etc. etc." Clearly he was urging us to give up everything.

It was known that when Rev. Abbé Duchesne, the learned, the "most learned" of men was frightened of a discovery which confused many of his theories, he had sent to Rev. Father, in February 92, a solemn and urgent letter.

Meanwhile, our Rev. Dupont had been to Paris, in July of the same year, '92. M. Fiat was pleased to receive him many times in private interviews, making him speak at length about Panaghia.. The same M. Fiat, three months later, had permitted Sister Grancey, without any objection, to buy Panaghia. We had registered with joy these two facts, as good precursors of a turnback in favour of Panaghia, and we were encouraged. Then we had taken advantage of this to publish this simple, popular booklet for the first time. I wrote to the Reverend late in December.

The reply came soon.

Paris, January 17, 1893

"I hasten to reply to your letter of 29th December, to inform you that my Council and I are absolutely in opposition to the publication of this booklet about the discovery of the Holy Virgin's House at Efesus. In consequence, I beg you to not to continue with this project. We have serious reasons for taking this decision, determined also by the statement of M. Duchesne, who is against you."

With such a formal Veto, we had our hands and legs bound. Should we give up Panaghia forever, and say farewell? It was now so far advanced it was not possible to turn back. What could we do? Look for some others to continue that we could not do anymore, to ignore this unfortunate opposition, to prove the evidence, or the weaknesses, the lack of reason, the emptiness put forward by the same Council and all the opposition that was to come?

We started to attack the opposition, and as M. Duchesne was the Principal, we started on him, with a letter dated 8th March '93, to the Rev. Allou, second Assistant of the Congregation, which was well documented.

M. Duchesne was so thoroughly defeated, he did not dare any more to oppose "his witness". Reverend Fiat himself came round in the end. I suppose he wished this personally, the good Reverend, it was his advisers who were hostile.

A solution had been found; the Council gathered ad hoc; his Excellency the Archbishop, M. Borrel etc. etc. had decided:

1) We would henceforth not appear in print;

2) His Excellency the Monsignor, and M. Borrel would be in charge of the booklet planned, one being the sponsor, and the bearer of public responsibility; the other would undertake to edit the booklet. Besides, a decision had been taken to wait for a more favourable time to publish it. We waited two years.

Meanwhile, we prepared some handwritten copies of the official Report of Enquiry to distribute when the occasion presented itself. Also, we composed (also by hand), a small, very small provisory notice about Panaghia's discovery in June '93. This was intended to inform the right people slowly, and easily, to diffuse the light well to places well chosen.

Early in '96, thinking the right moment had come, M. Borrel prepared the booklet.

He wrote about fifty pages; it remained unfinished, but this was not deliberate. We then took over the work ourselves. We determined our goal and plan: to state that we favoured only "Panaghia", and refute all arguments. The plan was to give an opinion to the reader after three chapters. Chapter III was important, because it contained the evidence, the proof. It was brief, clear and complete.

On 25th March '96, His Excellency signed the note to the reader. Between 25-29 March, Chapter I was quickly prepared. The note of '93 had been adapted, completed. That was all for this chapter. On March 29th we prepared Chapter II. On Wednesday, 28th April at 9 o'clock in the evening, the work was complete. It remained to write it out properly and send it for printing.

The following Friday, 17th April, the packet securely tied, was sent to France by registered post, to M. Oudin, one of our great Editors of Religion. To complete this popular booklet, and in order to interest the reader, to attract and charm, we wanted it to be illustrated with some views of Panaghia.

These would include the sites, the castle, mountain, the House, taken from the east, west, north, south etc. etc. But how could we send up there a graphic artist or a photographer? But there was another manifestation of Providence!

I was summoned to Constantinople for the Provincial Assembly. I had been there for some days, when M. Dumont wrote to me from Smyrna. What had happened to me again? "We have all our designs, done by professional artists, without any further expense." It was a Miracle! How had they done it? Upon my return, I had the answer to the enigma.

It was the first year of the Olympic Games. Three Frenchmen, artists and friends, had met by chance at these games: MMs. Pinchon, de la Néziéres, Avalot, all three of them reporters from some of the great daily newspapers of Paris: France Illustrée, Monde Illustré, Univers Illustré, and all three of them were charged with the artistic impressions. "Here, you!...And you!.., and you also!"

Very excited to meet in a stange land, they decided not to part, and to finish the journey together. "Where will we go after Greece? To Constantinople?" "No, let us go to Smyrna!" "Go to Smyrna!" Thus, our three artists disembarked on a beautiful day at Smyrna, in late April, '96.

At which hotel did they stay? That was less important. Going to the hall after dinner, they found "Le Courrier" on the table. By good luck that day "Le Courrier" contained news about Panaghia. Our friends read the article. They called the owner: "What is this Panaghia?" "It is a discovery made recently near Efesus; but I don't know much about it. If you wish to know more, contact M. Borrel, Director of the French Post Office, he will give you all the information you wish." Their curiosity awakened, our artists went directly to M. Borrel.

He received them as usual, with politeness. At the first word about Panaghia his face shone with a smile. "I will give you gentlemen all the details about Panaghia, the most reliable and detailed, being myself involved and one of the most convinced partisans. But let us do better! Let us go to the Lazarists College. Thereby you will see, you will hear the discoverer himself. Nobody could speak to you about Panaghia-Capoulou better than himself."

On their way to the College with M. Borrel, they went to Sacré Coeur..

M. Jung told them the history of Panaghia. He was so convincing that the three men, greatly impressed, choked back screams: "We must see that!"

"Very well, gentlemen!" said M. Borrel. "If you wish, I'll guide you." They accepted at once.

On April 28th, led by M. Borrel, they visited Panaghia, exploring the entire site at great length, as artists, pencils in hand. They came back on the 29th, charmed by their excursion, their souls rich with sights and impressions, and also plenty of drawings.

That is how, by a special favour of Divine Providence, without any trouble, or any expenses we obtained all our designs, executed by artists of the first order. Thank you, Good Providence! That was not all! To these designs was added an article about Panaghia signed by the three artists. One can read it on page 81 of the booklet about Panaghia-Capoulou.

I hastened to send these views to Oudin, and give the order he had waited for: "Do print."

Three months later, in mid September, '96, the booklet was printed in an edition of 5000 copies at a cost of 1400 Fr. without extras, postage, etc. It was the right moment this time to inform "urbi and orbi" of the Discovery: thus the booklet was distributed everywhere.

1) Bishopric: 90 copies to the Bishops, Archbishops and Cardinals of France and Algeria, 5 to those of Belgium, 2 to Luxembourg and Holland, 6 to England, Scotland and Ireland,- 10 to Spain, 4 to Portugal, 3 to Switzerland, 4 to Germany, 9 to Austria and Hungary and Poland, 10 to Italy and Sicily, 4 to Greece, 2 to Canada, 4 to the United States, 2 to Mexico, 4 to Peru, Brazil, Chili, the Republic of Argentina, etc.

2) Congregation: about twenty copies to Main House, 12 to the Community at Rue de Bac, 18 to the Visitors of the Little Company, 14 to the Superiors of our Great Seminaries in

France, 30 and more to various known Colleagues and specially chosen Sisters.

3) Five to Abbés and Superiors of Eudistes, to Foreign Missions, Pontigny, Staoueli, Pierre-qui-Vire.

4) Four to the great Catholic daily in Paris: "Le Monde", "L'Univers", "La Vérité", "La Croix",- 6 to the Religious Seminaries at Cambrai, Nantes, Orléans, Sens, Toulouse, Marseille, 1 to "L'Echo de Fourviéres", 1 to "L'Ami du Clerge" 1 to "Mois Bibliographique."

Also 225 copies had been sent to Constantinople and Smyrna, 169 to Sister Grancey to be distributed by herself here and there to parents, relatives, friends and the modest parishioners of the village; to Grancey's Gonteau-Biron, to Merode's, and to the Maréchale de Mac-mahon.

Nobody had been forgotten; neither Rev. Eschbach, nor Rome, nor M. Vigouroux of Saint-Sulpice, nor M. Duchesne of the Institute; nor the future Admiral Antoine, nor the good Brother Lievin, my pious and complaisant guide in Jerusalem etc. etc. etc. Like this, 600 and more copies of this work were sent all over the world. Others followed them.

Everywhere the Capouli booklet had succeeded in arousing curiosity, people would read avidly to find out what was real in this famous Discovery, the reverberations of which had diffused all over Europe. It obtained another success. Its modest, measured words, explaining things with simplicity without attacking anybody, firm, and frank, pleased both friends and enemies, and was well received and by all.

Some of the important personages deigned to thank us, by sending us cards with their best wishes.

The Archbishop of New York had read the work "With great pleasure" (25th August 96)

The Bishop of Scutari in Albania, speaking through the French Consulate, expressed in the same way his pleasure and his gratitude, (13th Oct. 96.)

Cardinal Manara, Bishop of Ancona, sent his card with his congratulations, his thanks and wishes for success.

Cardinal Sembrutovicz, Archbishop of Ruthenia, sent from Leopol "his most ardent thanks". (28th August 96)

Cardinal Steinberger wrote from Rome: "I was pleased to receive the booklet, "Panaghia - Capoulou", which I read with great interest, and I am happy that I have nothing against its well-established reasons. I wish this opinion to prevail." (5th September '96)

Cardinal Gotti, Chief-Administrator of Propaganda, "Received with pleasure and read attentively the booklet "Panaghia-Capouli" (20th October 1896.)

Among this concert of encouragement and favourable notices, no voice was heard in the press against the Booklet of Panaghia-Capouli

I am sorry! One voice was heard, the only one. This was of M. Berger, who had been carrying on a polemic against us since January '97. Nevertheless, he confirmed his good impression of the booklet. "All the primitive church, Jesus Christ, the Holy Virgin have always interested true Christians... Every time an unexpected discovery reveals something unknown until then, religious people are upset, and this spreads with rapidity. Infatuation is stronger if one includes in these narratives a famous visionary's Revelations."

"This is", he adds "What has happened with the discovery near Efesus, the ruins of a small church are claimed to be the Holy Virgin's House, where, according to C. Emmerich, she lived during the last years of her life and died surrounded by the Apostles. Many daily newspapers and magazines, not only in

Smyrna but also France, repeated this news and aroused great enthusiasm among some souls "surely more pious than learned."

In spite of the "dig" contained in the three last words, it had been recognised; we had registered.

When this good news arrived, we thanked God for this first success that he had accorded us. It was like a general approbation for all we had done until then. It was also an encouragement to continue the Catholic work we had started, to which God's Will had put us.

To end: this chapter of Panaghia-Capoulou was reported at the Marial Congress in Lyons, in September, 1900, in good terms.

Our little memoir was listened to with attention, and later had, with an Official Report, real approbation.

It was the same for the Marial Congress at Fribourg, two years after Lyons. Who represented Panaghia at this Congress and how? On what terms? I know only from a letter afterwards received that there, also -as a witness writes- the Efesus case made a good impression, and conquered the Doct Assembly as well.

I could say the same for the Marial Congress at Rome, in December, 1904, to celebrate the fiftieth anniversary of the Dogma of the Immaculate Conception. It was precisely the moment to speak about Panaghia's Discovery. Good persons insisted, pressed me to, M. Mott, M. Fiat, also. The last two wanted me to go to Rome to present the case and to plead for it.

I don't know, I disliked the idea at first, and for some time afterwards. Writing to Congress didn't appeal to me; going to Rome even less. I had no idea how to present it, nor how to treat the subject.

In November, 1904 M. Lobry summoned me to Constantinople, and took me with him to visit Macedonia. Meanwhile, he visited Salonica and Zeytinlik in his capacity of Visitor, and I rested quite well at the Seminary in Bulgaria. I was enjoying the sweetness of the rest and solitude. From my window I could see far away the gulf, Mt Olympus of Greece, its summit covered in snow, shining under the sun's rays. Could it be this ancient home of ancient Gods that inspired me? Or the rest and quietness that have given me again strength and ideas? I was thinking when a plan of Memorandum came to my mind, a beautiful and good plan. I hurried to write it down on paper and sent it off.

I was proud of my plan. Alas! I had forgotten that God does not like pride. Three weeks later I knew that this Memorandum would not have the honour to be presented at the Congress.

When I first heard, I wanted to shout and yell about injustice and partiality; the organiser of the Congress, Monsignor Radini Tadeschi, was not a supporter of Panaghia's case. I knew later that it was a general precaution taken by order of the Superior to remove, without partiality, anything that could be a cause of arguments and discussion. This consoled me.

We had lost a precious, incomparable opportunity to defend Panaghia's case before a tribunal representing the entire Catholic Universe; but one year later we were compensated, having aroused the interest of the Vatican and Rome in "The Grave of the Holy Virgin at Efesus".

Among all these controversies, Panaghia's case had made such progress in Rome in the souls of high ecclesiastical dignitaries, thanks to Rev, Eschbach, that since the year 1903 the Reverend Eschbach himself, with the support and encouragement of the Cardinal Vicar, his Excellency S.E. Parrochi, had prepared a project for a Roman Commission that would come and study in situ Panaghia's case. The great and famous Roman archeologist Marruchi had agreed to participate; the necessary funds for the journey's expenses were ready; the date of departure had been decided for the following Autumn, when the sudden death of Pope Leon XIII stopped everything suddenly.

We hoped this great Pope, who was so interested in Panaghia's case during his terrestrial reign, would continue to love and protect her in Heaven.

Chapter IX

The Controversies

The thesis we were preparing to defend and which we hoped would prevail had come up against many old prejudices without arousing violent protests.

How many good souls in some corners of the Latin Church firmly and quietly believed in the Jerusalem tradition, accepted it without question, without having even studied or verified its authenticity. It was worse for the Greek Orthodox Church. For thirteen centuries she had celebrated Mary's death at Jerusalem, for thirteen centuries she had preached through liturgical books, through her Fathers, the voices of learned men. It was almost a dogma, and all of a sudden the "dogma" was attacked, uprooted, and had collapsed like a ruined building. We had to be ready to expect numerous disputes and attacks.

Waiting for the attacks, we started meanwhile to attack ourselves. It has not been forgotten how the Abbot Duchesne, who honestly informed us in '92 - at the beginning of the Discovery-of his thoughts concerning the subject, had written in a hurry to set us against C. Emmerich and later he had written to the Reverend to set him against us. There had been implacable opposition from a learned man, which it was important to resolve. We started to attack from there.

Twelve months after my first letter to Abbot Duchesne, I wrote him a second letter on February 2nd, 1893, where I asked him two simple questions:

1)- What according to you, is the objection against Efesus?

2)- How would you explain logically the fact that C. Emmerich could so exactly describe a site, a house she had never seen, that no writer had ever spoken about?

I waited for his replies; they were more pitiful than I had supposed.

The First reply said: "All reasons against Efesus are reduced to one: a complete absence of tradition." What about the Efesus tradition which for centuries had rejected that of Jerusalem? The Second reply: "The similarity you refer to does not exist at all." Very well. Have we not eyes to see? The famous learned man sees better from his office than we who are actually there!

After these two replies, Abbot Duchesne was definitely defeated. Did he understand by himself? It seems to me that was so, after the obstinate silence he maintained. Emboldened by this first success and new studies, we dared, on 13th March, '96 to refer to a high and powerful personality, Monsignor Baunard, Rector of the Catholic University at Lille.

His Excellency Monsignor Baunard, it seems, in a St. John's Biography published in 1869, (reedited in '82 and very much appreciated), had supported the case for Jerusalem against Efesus. This involved him in some arguments with Monsignor Scappapietra, Archbishop of Smyrna; but this last event was not well documented, the argument was null and vaid.

"In spite of the charm of the legend which claims that Mary lived at Efesus," writes Mons. Baunard, "The critic must renounce this supposition, which is irreconcilable with tradition, chronology and history. According to severe and impartial truth, it is at Jerusalem..." What a beautiful phrase, Monsignor. How well it is said! But please answer a very small question. Tell us how the Efesus tradition is completely irreconcilable:

1) with the tradition, 2) with chronology, 3) with history; and how "according to" impartial and severe truth it is at Jerusalem etc. etc. Who was wrong ? The kind Prelate? He could assert, but when it came to proof, that was another matter!

Monsignor Baunard continued to assert that the Fathers "were unanimous" for Jerusalem. A second request: one, only one, if you please, Monsignor, one before the 6th century, before the ambitious Juvenal, who is responsible for it all!

V. Efesus or Jerus. p.p.113.117

Monsignor Beaunard did not correct his phrase; such a splendid phrase. He did not reply to our letter; he struck out his decisive assertion. "All the Fathers in unanimity claim..., etc..." You will not find it any more in the later editions.

After Monsignor Baunard, it was the turn of Rev. Le Camus, since then Monsignor Le Camus, who died recently as Bishop of La Rochelle. Monsignor Le Camus had written beautiful pages about Panaghia in his book "The Seven Churches", published in '96, but apart from these kind and beautiful pages, there are others which one does not know how to qualify. He starts with premises in favour of Efesus; but in conclusion, for purely childish reasons, he is against. Why is this? Maybe because of the discoverers, who in both circumstances did not show all the importance and attention owed towards his important and encumbering person. (S. Letters to Mons. Le Camus - Efes. or Jerus. pg. 124)

With him, victory was easy, it was enough to make out the illogicality of his conclusions, and put him against himself. He also received the "dig" without replying.

Three years later, in May '99, on his last visit Smyrna, M. Jung, with one word, but a terrible word, defeated him; "You claim, Reverend Camus, that the Holy Virgin did not die at Jerusalem, it is written at some length in the "Journey to the Biblical Countries". You claim also that she did not die at Efesus; it is written in your. "Book of Seven Churches..." Well! Let us admit that she died at Mecca, and put an end to this dispute". A loud Homeric laugh followed this joke. Mons. Le Camus tried to laugh with the others, but evil tongues say it was a hollow laugh.

While we were engaged in minor battles with Rev. Duchesne, and Mons. Baunard, another important and serious enemy launched a campaigh against us; the Patriarch of the Orthodox Church in Jerusalem, who defended his traditions through his mandatory, the respected Professor Chrysostomos Papadopoulos.

The attack was polite, the justification clever, all well written, rich in citations. There is only one fault in this brilliant defence; many of the assertions or arguments are baseless, so all is null and void.

The booklet printed in Jerusalem, in mid '96, is summarised by four propositions: 1) Saint John did not come to Efesus before A.D 64. -2) The Holy Virgin, being 80 years old, could not follow him to Asia. 3) The letter of the Council says that the temples of Saint John and the Holy Virgin were not dedicated to Saint John himself or to the Holy Virgin Herself. 4) Many Fathers affirm that the Holy Virgin never left Jerusalem.

We pointed out very respectfully to the Very Reverend Patriarch and his mandatory, the respected Chrisostomos Papadopoulos, that all the testimonies they presented, taken one by one, did not prove their thesis. We showed them the fragility of their propositions. Ad. I- Where was John in A.D 38-40 and 64? Why should only one of the Apostels wait fifteen years after the Holy Virgin's death and thirty years after that of the Saviour to undertake the Holy Spirit Mission, since according to the pious Fathers he had been especially summoned at the start? Ad. 2) According to the apocryphers, if it is true the Saint John came to Asia Minor earlier, why, then, did the Holy Virgin not follow him ? Ad. 3) Never had the Council referred to John briefly or to Mary, when referring to the church of Saint John or the Church of Holy Mary. Or in the text in question, it says only "John" and "Mary"; so it means this is about persons, not about churches. Ad. 4) For the reason that there are so many Fathers in Jerusalem, it would not be difficult for Reverend Chrisostomos Papadopoulos to quote us some, would it?

Only one, please, to him: only one! Before 451. S.Efes.Jer.p.127-129.

We sent our reply to Patriarch Gerasimus I; since then we have not heard from their side.

Meanwhile, while we were arguing with Jerusalem's Orthodoxies, a polemic started at Smyrna on the same subject, between the Orthodoxies of Smyrna and vicinity.

It was the Bishop of Heliopolis, Monsignor Tarasios, who put the fat in the fire through "Amalthia" of 24th April, (6th May) '96.

He claimed that the Holy Virgin did not die at Efesus and had never been there.

This was the doctrine "of the Orthodox Church of the Orient; the unique true Catholic, apostolic church, column and base of the Truth, charged with governing and teaching universality to believers, being the ultimate and divine interpreter, both for the Holy Scriptures and for sacred traditions".

One of our young Catholics took up the defence proudly.

M. Diamandopoulos, professor at the school of Ahgia Photini, intervened in the debate. After M. Diamandopoulos came the Rev. Chrysostomos, Archdeacon of the Efesus Metropol. The Fener Patriarchate of Constantinople lined itself up, publishing in "Alithia Ecclissiastiki", its official newspaper, on 17th May, No. 12, an unpleasant article qualifying Panaghia's discovery as a "fairy myth" and "papist action".

Our young Catholic M. Emile Lorentz argued courageously against Mr. Diamandopoulos first, later against Rev. Chrisostomos. It was a pleasure to see the fair replies he threw in the faces of his adversaries.

For many weeks, attacks and replies were published in "Amalthia" with ardour.

More than twenty articles had been published. At last the Greek newspapers stopped publishing Mr. Lorentz' replies, on the pretext that he had written so many articles, and of lack of space, so finally they stopped. Only some letters or articles in defence of their champion, the Archdeacon Hrisostomos, appeared.

Under these conditions, M. Lorentz had to retire; so he did. He left the Rev. Chrisostomos to fight and triumph all alone.

Three things remained from this polemic: 1) the recognition by our adversaries of the deep impression made on the whole Christian world, Orthodoxies, Catholics and Protestants, by Panaghia's Discovery. 2): The evident, tangible weakness of the Orthodox adversary's thesis. They had for them only the apocryphers or suspicious authorities, baseless arguments without any logic; audacious, arrogant and empty assertions. To compose a work! What a style! Good heavens!

An example of their arguments: "Study of the Apostles deeds, chapter XVIII until chap. XXI. These chapters establish clearly that St. Paul was the first Apostle to come to Efesus; neither St. John, nor God's Mother, nor any other Apostle came before him. (-"Amalthia," 6-18 June 96). Yes! Go and see!

An example of the way they are reasoning: three, four, five columns in the newspaper, full of great words but insubstantial; long, pompous, high-sounding but empty phrases; sharps assertions but without proof, all of which was meant to mean: part I: You are ignorant, I am learned; I will crush and annihilate you. Part II: I have crushed, pulverised, and annihilated you.

You are conquered and I triumph:

This is an example of style, particularly of the Rev. Chrisostomos, the principal defender of "sacred traditions". He threatens to extinguish them in a huge, inexhaustible ocean of historic testimonies and scriptures.

He boasts! "The magnificent edifice of his doctrines and wise knowledge". He continues: "The splendid edifice of written testimonies, historical facts, has risen up and proved it. Instead of losing, he is covered with radiance and strength and strength, more manifest, more undisputable, because of the complete aphasia and sad silence of the noble adversaries, who have turned round because of mountains inaccessible for them, and his uncontestible chronological calculations, based on the Scriptures".

In some parts he compares M. Lorentz to "an eel that slithers to escape from his strong and uncontestable reasons." In another he speaks of Lorentz as "a man who trusts in the fragile body of his personal opinion, which is absolutely without any defence, that is completely ignorant about the question and attacks an antagonist armed from top to toe, that he is filled with pity for him!" (See "L'Amalthia", 8-20 June 96.)

Nevertheless, nothing is comparable to the sublime phrase cited yet elsewhere of the Doct professor Diamandopoulos, who "takes in hand truth's hammer, sometimes history's heavy axe to strike the terrible lie on the head!" "The inconsistency and false hypothesis!" "All the bastard publications "and finally," With the help of the evil, papist church, which tries "to mislead" the good Orthodox Church, on the occasion "of the incoherent dreams" of C. Emmerich and the claimed marvellous discovery of Panaghia Capoulou." (Amal. 16 June 96.)

To retain to the end of these polemics the precious recognition in 'Amalthia' of 8-20 April 96, Pdo. 5954, regarding the Greek tradition in favour of the Holy Virgin's death at Panaghia Capoulou. We give the article literally translated. Read it and take note seriously. Never you will find it under the Greeks' pen, though!

"Very often has been question about Panaghia-Capouli, a place situated between Kirkindji and New Efesus been raised. This place is considered "sacred" by "our" people, who in consequence light a lamp.

There was a time when Catholic priests bought it from an Ottoman who was the owner, in order to build a sanctuary to honour the Holy Virgin, who as tradition says, died up there."

After we had finished with all these small battles, we were resting peacefully on our laurels, when a new attack took place, from whom we were least expecting it. It was not Greek, but it was quite worthy to be.

Towards March' 97, six months after the Panaghia booklet was published, I received by post directly from Paris a copy of "L'Echo" monthly of the Holy Land, the March number. From whom had it been sent and why? I opened it and I understood. A long letter dated January, nine pages against C. Emmerich and Panaghia-Capouli, its discoverers and their supporters. "Sincere souls and in good faith" without any doubt, but of course, "more pious than erudite".

I did not know from whom this unexpected aggression had come. I took my pen at the same moment and in a fluent hand I replied to "L'Echo." It was a good reply, which put things in their right place, and re-established the truth as texts and facts as well.

In the following months, there were new letters, repeating with unperturbed assurance the wrong information contained in the preceding letters, without any attention being paid to our corrections, going on as if nothing had happened. Oh, what loyalty! Should we feel offended? Not reply any more? Take it easy! Good mouse, good cat! At every new letter, I replied immediately; but my reply was thrown in the waste paper basket. In spite of my claims, in spite of many promises, never, not even once, did the monthly "L'Echo" of the Holy Land publish, or even mention them.

The author, signed J. Berger, was an unknown name to us. After the third letter and some precise details I suspected who the man was. Doubt soon became certitude.

Late in '93 we had celebrated in Constantinople the quinquegenary of Rev. Regnier, former Director of the Sisters, former Superior of St. Benoit and Dean of the Province. In February' 94 M. Lobry took him to Smyrna. We took the venerable old man out, of course we visited Aidin, Efesus and Panaghia.

In those days the Rev. Arséne du Chatel, ex-provincial of Capouchins at Versailles, familiar with us and well-known by M. Lobry, who had the occasion to meet him very often at St. Louis at Constantinople lodged at St. Polycarpe for a while. This good man, who knew about the arrival of MM. Lobry and Régnier in Smyrna and had heard about the trip to Panaghia, imagined ingenuously that he could come as well. He had not made his wish known to any of us, also, it was a family celebration; we did not even think of inviting him. The good Father was offended greatly.. et inde iras.

He said next day to Sister Grancey: "I hoped they would take me also but they didn't; I'm finished with the Lazarists," and making the gesture fit the words he flapped his hands, like a man who says: "quite good friends". Since that moment, without changing his relationship with us, his old friendliness had changed to hostility, hardly dissimulated, almost open against Panaghia. He went by himself to Panaghia, under bad conditions for us, and lodged objections against the Efesus thesis.

It was he, who after three years of rancour, when he returned to France, took advantage of the publication of the Panaghia booklet to vent his anger under his patronymic, unknown at Smyrna: J. Berger.

Once it was known who he was, we ceased to reply. We did well; but of what importance was it for M. Berger? "L'Echo" continued to publish his letters and pass over ours in silence. The good M. Berger triumphed! Wait, M. Berger!

When M. Berger had sufficiently triumphed over us, to emphasise his victory he had the audacity to publish in booklet form his five or six letters to L'echo without correcting the errors pointed out to him and properly described by us. Alas! His enjoyment did not last long. Almost as soon as: "Efesus or Jerusalem" appeared, our five letters to M. Berger were printed. (Page 139.) They demolished the false science of M. Berger, his apparent goodness, his suspect assertions, his false judgement and his rancour against this or that. Who stopped laughing? M. Berger, who felt totally defeated.

Poor M. Berger. I had the occasion to see him again once more. Passing through Smyrna for Constantinople, he could not go without seeing me. He came only for one little minute, and stood in the parlour; so precisely, as if to the last stroke of the clock. Monsignor was waiting for me in the sacristy for the Pontifical Vespers of the 3rd day of 40 hours. How red in the face he was! How constrained he seemed! I went up to him with a kind smile, without any bad thought. After all, I was against his writings, not against him... Besides, had I not been satisfied?

It is said that on his death-bed M. Berger apologised courteously for his unkind actions against Panaghia. Others also did it for him, frankly nobly.

The Reverend Father Moyse, a Capouchin from Lyons, Procuror of the Missions in the Orient had came to Smyrna to preach during Lent, 1899. He wished, during his stay, to visit Panaghia, in order to understand for himself. He asked me almost shyly for permission. "Oh Father! Surely you can go and see as much as you wish!" "If M. Jung could come with me, it would be a great favour, I should be very grateful to you." M. Jung, being free, went with him and other religious of St. Polycarpe, whom he had taken with him.

The next day, Wednesday 1ˢᵗ March 1899, late evening was at my window when they returned. I saw Rev. Moyse and M. Jung cross the courtyard and go straight to the Cabinet of Physical studies. "Here!" thought I, "Without saying anything to me!" I was still thinking about it when someone knocked at my door. "Come in!" I saw Rev. Moyse, who came in without his two colleagues. He took my hand, deeply moved, with tears in his eyes and voice. "Thank you, Reverend Superior, for the grace you have accorded me. I had no right after all that happened. I wish to put things right, that is the reason I am here at this hour with my two colleagues. Forgive me, forgive me in the name of all the Order!"

Dear Father Moyse! On his return to the city he said to his colleagues; "You, go to the convent to leave the luggage; then come back quickly to College. We have a duty of justice to pay back, and I wish to do so before I return to St. Polycarpe." That is why in spite of presenting himself first to me, he went to M. Jung to wait for his colleagues.

Later he described to me his joy at visiting Panaghia, his deep conviction that it was really Mary's House. "It is marvellous", he repeated, "Everything is there!" Then, his heart overflowing with what he had seen, he said: "I will go back to France, I will speak; I will speak and I will unveil duplicities and lies."

He kept his promise. In many circumstances I needed him for our cause, every time he behaved like a good and fervent friend of Panaghia.

The Greek Patriarch of Jerusalem had said his word; the Patriarch of Constantinople did the same; the Orthodox Church of Smyrna, M. Berger and the others. Was it not the moment to say also our word? To say it out loud, in order that all the world could hear? Yes, we thought about and an idea for a new booklet came up: "Efesus or Jerusalem", destined to illuminate public opinion, to lead us gently but strongly, free souls, by the only fact of the known truth. Started on 20ᵗʰ

February, 1897, completed in June, delivered to be printed on the 29th of the present month, it appeared on 29th September.

It was a genuine booklet of debate, in spite of looking merely pleasant. It had a preface to establish briefly but firmly: 1) there were in the Church and history two traditions about the place where the Holy Virgin died: Efesus and Jerusalem. To establish 2) that the Efesus tradition was as old as that of Jerusalem. To establish: 3) The Efesus tradition had replaced that of Jerusalem, even if did not threaten to outweigh it. Then came two parts: First, Jerusalem. All Jerusalem's authorities were evaluated and determined. Second part: Efesus: it was the same, they were determined and evaluated. To end: as malicious appendices there was the Rev. Duchesne's letter, our letter to Monsignor Baunard, our letter to Mons. Le Camus, all our letters to Rev. Berger that "L'Echo" had prudently forgotten to publish. There were also other letters written to reply to particular objections, to better clarify everything that had not been placed in the context in this piece of work.

The whole was signed with the nom-de-plame: Gabrielovich. That is my real name, oriental as I am, son of Gabriel; but its exotic style covered me, too, kept me out of view.

The book was set out honestly and clearly, evaluated with its true worth. The reader was free to make his own conclusion, to choose between Jerusalem or Efesus. Nevertheless, the general meaning of the booklet disposed for Efesus.

With its correct and frank proceedings, its simple and strong reasons, its always clear discussion, always courteous, always rigorous, its clear and consistent style, "Efesus or Jerusalem" caused a sensation in the Christian world. For many, it was a discovery; for the common people, friend or enemy, an event. Never had the two traditions: "Jerusalem or Efesus" been studied so seriously, within their context.

Never had anyone searched right back to their origins to prove the truth, strong or weak.

Soon testimonies arrived from everywhere, for the most part full of satisfaction, the most sincere congratulations, the warmest wishes for the entire and prompt success of our work. Religious of different Orders, high level laics, Superiors of Communities, Professors of Great Seminaries, Rectors of Catholic Faculties, Bishops, Archbishops, Cardinals, etc. etc.. Hereby I have to hand their cards and letters:

I keep them with care as good testimonies of the work already done, also as encouragement for the work that remains to be done.

Among the testimonies of satisfaction and congratulations then received, the dearest among all was that of the Reverend Father Fiat, our General Superior. He had the kindness to write me a special letter on this occasion. This letter is so eulogistic, I would not like to speak about it. Otherwise, there is such a sudden change in favour of Panaghia, I cannot but quote. It goes as follows:

"Paris, 1 October 1897. I have just read a part and glanced through the rest of "Efesus or Jerusalem." I feel the necessity of expressing my satisfaction with this booklet, which interested me greatly. It has been for you a work of research and critique, which honours both you and yours for all you did to elucidate this question, and provoke a religious movement towards Panaghia-Capouli.

May the Immaculate Mother repay you and yours a hundred fold for the work done for Her.

I am ....etc...."

How far we are from the controversies of 91-93! When we remember the defiance and prohibitions of the first years; when we remember that the Rev. Mailly, who was sent to Constantinople and Salonica in July '93 as Extraordinary Commissary, had among his instructions, the suspicious order to go to Panaghia to clarify this "affair".

Reading the letter of the Reverend, we admire and bless God for the progress made.

The newspapers quickly got hold of the Booklet and spread the news all over the world.

For our part, we distributed a lot of copies to the five Continents of the world. In Europe: France, Spain, Belgium, England, Switzerland, Germany, Austria, Greece and Macedonia. In the Americas: Canada, the United States, Mexico, Brazil, Chile. In Africa: Algeria, Tunis, Egypt, Madagascar,

In Asia: Turkey, Syria, Palestine, even China and Pekin. In Oceania: to the Chiefs of Missions who asked for it. This time we addressed copies especially to the notables: of science, in the Church, notables of the publishing world; and to the high schools, the Universities of Paris, of Lyons, of Lille, of Antwerp, Fribourg, Innbruck, Iena, Louvain, Malines, of Washington, of Cambridge, Oxford, etc. etc. At Oxford our little volume had the honour to be placed in the Library of Honour. (Rector's letter).

Among the newspapers which gave space to the new booklet, some announced it in flattering terms; others analysed, summarised and gave the most favourable reports.

To quote some of the main examples:- "L'Ami du Clerge," of 4 November' 97, an excellent analysis of the work concludes like this. "Anyone who rejects Efesus before reading M. Gabrielovich's work, is ignorant of the subject matter of the critic." To cite "La Revue des Revues" which, through the pen of M. Boyer D'Agen, publishes entire extracts of "Efesus or Jerusalem," with views of Panaghia, and he himself acts as a supporter of our cause.

A newspaper from Chile "Le Porvenir" does the same under the pen of the distinguished M. Martinez, several times President of Council, of ministries, and Chief of the Catholic Party. "Le

Tiempo" from Mexico, prints M. Martinez's article in its entirety and adopts all the conclusions.

To cite "l'Univers," La Libre Parole," "La Jeunesse de Bordeaux," "Le Patriote de Bruxelles," "Le Patriote de Normandie," "Le Standard de Londres," etc. etc.

To finish with the illustrious and erudite "Civilta Catholica," which in a very long study of 16 April '98, recognises without hesitation that, after the booklet "Efesus or Jerusalem", the tradition of Hierossolimytism is ended. To accept definitely the Efesus tradition, it asks to know one thing: for it to be proved that Brentano had not seen or copied, that he only knew from C. Emmerich herself.

A quantity of Religious Weeks have been organised in France and have echoed in the famous newspapers: "Semaine de Nancy," "Semaine de Verdun," "Semaine de Perigueux," "Semaine de Rouen," "Semaine de Paris," "La Rochelle," "Echo de Fourviaeres," etc. etc...

Who has been unpleasantly surprised by the publication of our booklet? The group of the so-called learned. They were utterly bewildered. Who, outside of the erudite group could claim to have an historical opinion of this importance and dare to affirm it?

M. Dorme, one of our people, possessed a brilliant intellect with which that of the "learned men" compared unfavourably. The affect was as by a stone thrown into a pool of frogs! We could not stop there! Come! Courage! Everyone took up his old weapon to attack! One, his old rapier, another, his ancient blunderbuss.

But when we found ourselves confronted by the enemy, we perceived that our old rapiers and blunderbusses would not be sufficient in front of their modern artillery! The able and the malicious soon retire prudently, leaving to the less farsighted the glory of attacking and the unpleasantness of defeat.

At the head of the able, I shall name Rev. Lagrange, the well-known head of the Dominican School in Jerusalem. Rev. Legrang had been visiting our Brotherhood at Alexandria when they received the booklet. He turned the pages with irritation:... "I will answer! I will answer!" he screamed loudly. Since then, ten years have passed since Rev. Lagrange's nice display of agitation.

Since then he has inspired opposition, led those who write against Panaghia, but there is no word from himself, absolutely nothing. I am still looking for a word, a line signed by him attacking Panaghia, a reason to reply.

All did not have his circumspection. Beware! The first who darted his small arrow was Rev. de la Broise S.J, an excellent man by the way, and deeply religious. His stroke was like a Jesuit's. Instead of gettinghis mind clear about the essay, "Efesus or Jerusalem", he read quickly, too quickly; after which the thunderbolt fell! "When they emphasise St. Paul's and his first disciple's ignorance about St. John's stay in the city, they reply: what is there to be astonished about! St. Paul was in the city... and St. John was up in the mountains with his colony, three leagues away"...Three leagues! Just imagine!

It is as easy to put down an adversary as it is to make him say what he did not, and to make him look ridiculous. Gabrielovich was awakened. At once a letter was sent from Smyrna to Jersey to importune the kind Father! Pardon, dear Father! On which page of the booklet do they read what you make him say? I supposed that M. Gabrielovich gave everywhere as the real reason not St. Paul's ignorance but his silence about the others, as the latter used to say: "Non enim audeo loqui eorum quae per me non efficit Christus." (Letter of 3 December 97)

The good Father La Broise was caught! He became red in the face, bowed his head; later he admitted frankly his error and he did not speak any more.

Since then we have been in correspondence, arguing courteously. He sends me his objections, I send him my reply. I was pleased to see him at every meeting, losing, tumbling, down. As the illustrious Michel Morin said; "de brancha, in brancham degringolat que facit pouf". He has not yet got to "pouf" but he is near, as he waits the Grave's discovery to be given up.

A more serious attack and let us say, more authorised attack came from Corsica in 1899. The author was a learned priest. A professor of theology, a "familiar of Leon XIII", member of the Association of Academies Pontificates Tiberina, Arcadia, Romana also of the Society of Jurisconsults, Rev. Pieraccini...Very moderate, very correct in form, perfectly reasoned and suited, this thesis had a fault and was wrong from the start. It is in Latin, in order, says the author, to be read by more people.

Rev. Pieraccini proceeds in modo scholastic; he puts together the subject. He takes all centuries, one after the other, for every century he cites testimonies in Jerusalem's favour.

First century: Denys Aeropagyte. 2nd century: Eliton of Sardes and Polycrate from Efesus. 3rd century: St. Epiphany. 4th century: St. Athanasins's sermons, those of Sophron, of St. Augustine, 5th century: Juvenal of Jerusalem. 6th century: Gregory of Tours. 7th century: St. André of Crete. 8th century: St. John of Damascus.- 9th century: Nicephorus, Strabon de Foulde. 10th century: Fulbert de Chartres, etc. etc.

It is like a strong army, which moves, in good discipline, sure that nothing can resist. When someone does not like think himself, he ignores the question. There is really something imposing, I understand, that impersonates the soul of a new reader, it outweighs every other conviction.

Indeed, it is like a house of cards: blow and it falls down. All these false authorities have cited in favour of Jerusalem since the first century until the tenth, either apocryphers and most others, they say what they want them to say: like St. Epiphany, St. Gregoire de Tours and many others. Nothing is easier than to disprove the work completely, writing forever with authority: nego, so probetur... Do prove! Until you prove, I declare your authority, your assertions to be false!

Pieraccini worked consciously on his thesis, but he had not, like us, done ten years of continuous research about the same subject. He took a brilliant appearance for the truth, but he was wrong... My respects to these unlucky adversaries, but they are loyal and sincere!

We had two other attacks to sustain this year: one from the Rev. Germer-Durand, Assumptionist of Notre-Dame of France, the other from the Abbot Heydet, priest of the Latin Patriarcate, both of them from Jerusalem.

The Rev. Germer-Durand, well known for his work about Palestine, published in 1899 two articles against Panaghia; one in "Les Echos d'Orient", the other "Les Missions Catholiques". He gave three conferences which have not been published. I am not sorry because it disgusts me to get involved in regrettable and sterile polemics. (Letter 28 April 99).

If I didn't know otherwise, if I were not sure that Rev. Germer is a dignified and honest religious man, what wouldn't I think about him after letter like this! Good heavens, Father Germer! He shrinks from getting involved in a regrettable and sterile polemics. He attacks first, and he attacks two printed articles and three published conferences. Why does he attack if he does not like one's replies to him?

It was some days later, after this strange reply, when the always good and attentive Providence put in my hands a number of "Annales de Sion", March 99. This number started with an official report about the conferences of Rev. Germer-Durand. The Father's whole thesis was: "the Efesus tradition is all recent and refers to Catherine Emmerich:"

With this document, I was indeed powerful. I replied to Rev. Germer: "You say the tradition is all recent... Benedictus XIV speaks about it in the 18th century, Hippolite the Thebain in the 10th century Helecca from Saragossa in the 8th; is all this recent? - You say that he refers to C. Emmerich. I should like to know how Benedictus XIV in the 18th century, Hippolyte the Thebain in the 10th century Helecca in the 8th could refer to C. Emmerich, who died only in 1824?

What could one reply? Thus, the poor Rev. Gerber limited his ambition by pleading extenuating circumstances, sent me the newspaper which, said he, developed his thoughts better. Four or five years later I had a second affair like this with Rev. Gerber, about the map of Cadaba, or rather about the commentary he published. He begins by establishing a principle: one cannot identify any monument as Jerusalem, except maybe the Holy Sepulchre; later obviously by the word Geth... It is the Holy Virgin's Grave, declares he. Eh! Father, what about your principle, right now? What do you think of that? Have you forgotten?... And also, why the Virgin's Grave rather than the Cave of Agony? What about the Garden of Gethsemane? Have you the documents concerned? Being pressed to explain, Rev. Gerber accepted his weakness and retracted graciously. (See his letter, 27 Oct.1904) Yes. But what is written is written; people who buy the map of Madaba will see written on it the Virgin's Grave.

Abbot Heydet is a palestinologist of merit. He collaborated for M. Vigouroux's great Biblical Dictionnary. An honest man, too! Deeply disgusted, also, to see people without the knowledge to attack a tradition, the only founded, the only true, the only authentic, the only old, the only universal and cherished one He attacked with all his strength. The poor fellow! But let us start from the beginning, "ab ovo".

Late October 1999, Rev. Mott from Paris, going for his retirement to the Clergy at Jerusalem, passed through Smyrna. I made use of the opportunity: "Dear Rev. Mott, you will be for many weeks in enemy land, among them. I pray you, collect!

Collect all you can hear, see, and objections against Efesus and Panaghia. There is nothing as good as objections to clarify any question; nothing better to defend a cause, and establish it on an immovable base.

Next November 14th , Rev. Mott was again in Smyrna, on his way back to France. He gave me a booklet and a manuscript. What a piteous air he had! "Here", said he, "Are the objections you asked me for, there is more than you wish." "Why more, dear Reverend Mott? Are we not looking for truth? If they convince us, we will accept. Long live truth! But I deeply believe it will be as in the past: it will be the same, with new objections, but they will melt as snow under the sun!"

Good Rev. Mott was far from sharing our trust. He had heard so much against us at Jerusalem from all mouths and all colours and all kinds and all sizes. He had promised to himself to go to Panaghia, thence his passage in October. Shaken in his primitive faith, he did not dare to. To hide his retreat if not his defection, he pleaded the need to see someone in Constantinople. We had to smile.

But let us see this booklet and this manuscript. My booklet was in fact Rev. Pieraccini's, known and ordered by myself. It was a relief for Rev. Mott when he knew that, he began to hope again. I am not sure if he regretted having missed Panaghia.

I started with the manuscript. It was Rev. Haydet's work. He started with the discoverers, the defenders, the propagators of Panaghia-Capouli. "To prove that God's Mother died at Efesus... they offered us a salad of arguments... Let us proceed to clear up a little the elements, in order to be able to enumerate and estimate them at their real value."

After this thoughtless beginning, he attacks our authority: "People of the 16th century, of the 17th century, of the 18th century! Here," he clamours with arrogance "are testimonies of those who have seen and are competent!" He gives then his own authorities. They are these we already know, and we so often had the occasion to destroy, them.

To finish, a stroke of the tam-tam and big drum; let us say politely, a pathetic élan! "To attack a tradition fifteen centuries old, based upon thousands of testimonies presented by all the most holy and learned in the world and agreed by all Churches? To risk throwing discredit upon all the Holy Land's traditions...To expose the supernatural, the Revelations, the authority of the head of the church to the unbelievers' derision!...To expose to ruin faithful spirits!.. All this for the triumph of a scholar's whim, guaranteed by the authority of a poor and ignorant Greek peasant. A funeral joke! Criminal outrage!"

Replies swiftly followed in the case of the three repartees. The repartee at the disdainful beginning: "A salad of arguments....etc."

It it thus pleases Rev. Heydet of the Latin Patriarchate in Jerusalem to so qualify the booklet "Efesus or Jerusalem'. "It is enough to clarify the elements..." You qualify M. Gabrielovich's work as embroiling, M. Abbot? Let me say to you that the Reverendissime Rector of the Catholic Institute in Paris does not think like you.

"All that I read pleased me very much," writes he... "A perfect exposition". Letter to Monsignor Péchanard, 16 September 97.

Repartee to principal attack: Our testimonies did not see; did yours see more? Our testimonies have at least the authority of those who studied the subject deeply and know. Yours, what authority have they? All apocryphers, or based upon apocryphers.

Final Repartee: "If we ruin faith, if our tendency is criminal, then the great and learned Pope Benedictus XIV said and did that before us. We say and continue to do so after him...A Pope...one of the most esteemed Popes, who ruins the faith and allows criminal tendencies! Poor Roman Church! Fortunately the Greek Schismatic Church is there to save it! There now, M. Abbot! Where are you leading with your exaggerations!

Poor Abbot Heydet certainly didn't wait to be defeated. Under this stroke, he bent back and shoulders, and as he was loyal and frank he accepted it all without rancour.

To the extent that he was arrogant and sarcastic in his factum, as he says himself, in letters written to me later he was just as polite, sweet and modest. He ended this letter asking for permission to continue keeping "a belief dear to his heart". (Note: and he kept it, being resentful about Efesus. Cf. Supplement of Bible Dic., word Assumption).

Many copies of our reply to the Abbot Heydet have been taken and sent to the right places; the French Benedictines of Jerusalem, Rev. Eschbachat of Rome, our colleagues in Constantinople, to Rev. Abbot Moreau, to Rear Admiral Antoine, to Rev. Mott and Rev. Vigouroux in Paris. Rev. Vigouroux approved this reply, "proved that Jerusalem failed". Rev. Mott pressed me to publish it. I agreed for the moment, but I needed to give time to Rev. Heydet to publish his attack against our reply, and also give him the opportunity of reviewing his manuscript and of cancelling everything that incorrect. As for the corrections of his manuscript, he was so conscientious that he let us to do it. For various reasons it took time, dragged out and never reached the end.

Rev. Heydet's attack served for a very precious discovery. Looking in the books and old papers in order to reply to M. Duchesne and Mons. Baunard, we noticed that all authorities on Jerusalem referred to Juvenal and stopped at Juvenal; there was nothing before Juvenal. Searching again in "Fathers and Learneds" to establish who was for Efesus and who for Jerusalem, we remarked something new. While in the Orient, Fathers, Learneds, historians and Churches since 7th century had all enthused for Jerusalem, whereas in the West the Latin Church was silent, absolutely silent, a deliberate silence. - (See

Grave of H.V. at Efesus, page 168 and foll;) Fathers and Learneds speak about the Holy Virgin's death, but as for the place, they are silent, they pass over it with minds open. This is particularly seen in Gregoire of Tours. What he says about the Holy Virgin's death is taken from the Apocryphers; but strangely, in all the details taken he leaves the place out of his narration. It is clear, the Roman Church never accepted Jerusalem's tradition. What a reference for Efesus!

We had the satisfaction of knowing the question was going further. "Do you know Diario Romano? Ordo Romano asked me one day about Monsignor Thomas, ex-Delegate in Persia in our College." "No, Monsignor." "But it is just for you."

I looked at the Ordo, what did I see? This notice of 15 August: the Virgin Mary died at Efesus-as the best-based opinion.

Looking for information, I knew this notice had been in the Ordo since 1890; so that was before the discovery, and in consequence was not clear! The Roman Church, always so prudent concerning Efesus or Jerusalem, was for Efesus.

I enjoyed this notice of the Diario, I quoted it willingly to our adversaries. One day it disappeared from the Ordo. Who took it? I accused those who supported Jerusalem, particularly Abbot Duchesne, of having something to do with it. Then I found out in a sure way that it was simply the new editor of Ordo, who had taken it off by himself without any malice. That is good for us; in 1904, after observations had been made, the said notice was at once put again in the new Roman Ordo, after an order on the purpose of the Cardinal Vicar as the Pope's order. Oh, blessed suppression which should have such a good result and so blessed a re-establishment!

(-See letters P. Eschbach, 18 March 1903.)

While we argued in the Orient and France, a Venerable Canon argued in Germany; the Learned Nirschl Dean of the Cathedral and Chapter House of Wurzbourg. In 1894 he published a first booklet against Panaghia and Efesus, a second in '96, a third in 1900. These three booklets were in German, it was difficult to reply.

Thus, we left it to Rev. Schnoeger, Rev. Wegener, and Rev. Fonck, and at last Rev. Abbot Niessen, Chaplain of St. Adalbert at Aix-la-chapelle. We made them withdraw all the objections we were able to and we disproved them when the occasion presented itself.

All we know is that these opuscules are different appreciations of opuscules Like Rev. Barnabe, Nischl proves "magisterially" that the Holy Virgin died at Jerusalem. As for Rev. Pelt of Metz "his theses hold up better than those of his adversaries". As for Rev. Fonck, well-known among the Learned of Germany and himself knowing the Rev. Nischl: "The best we can say to discharge the kind Rev. Nischl, is that he is over 80 years old, he is not able to distinguish truth from fiction" (Letter of Rev. Fonck to Monsignor Timoni.)

The Abbot Niessen, in a voluminous book published in 1906, revised all the arguments again, all objections, all the difficulties of Doct. Nirschl; it was not hard for him to establish and discover sometimes emptiness, sometimes suspicion.

From 1899 to 1903 there was no battle nor even debate of any importance; only some attacks from here and there, some hidden, without waiting for any reply. How many letters I had to write sometimes to reply to a newspaper article or review, sometimes to summarise a report or Bibliography more or less exactly, sometime to correct false assertions or reply to particularl objections, to clarify partial difficulties. I counted more than twenty. A letter to Rev. Husson of Main House, letter to Rev. Pieraccini from Corsica, letter to the Learn. Nirschl of Wurzbourg, letter to Fath. Sejourne of St. Etienne of Jerusalem, letter to Fath. Hilaire, Fransiscan from Paris, letter to the Abbot Pisani, professor at the Catholic Institute of Paris,- many letters to Father de la Croise, letters to the Abbot Heydet. A second letter to Mons. Baunard, letter to l'Ami du Clerge, letter to Father of Smedt, Director of Bollarists, Brussels. Letter to M. Rouhart, professor at the Catholic Faculty at Lille, letter to Mons. Terghien, for his "Mother of God", letter to Director de la Couronne de Marie.

Lyons: letter to Abbot Lesetre, collaborator in Rev. Vigouroux's Biblical Dictionary, letter to Father Liernard, French Benedictans in Jerusalem, letter to M. Milon, general Secretary of Lazarists, letter to Fath. Memain. Canon at Sens, letter to Rev. Lorenzo, Superior of Capuchins at Boudja, letter to Abbot Turmel, collaborator La Revue du Clerge, letter to M. Hebert, correspondent of "L'Univers" and "Le Monde,"- Letters to M. Correspondent and editor "La Croix" etc. etc.

The big war seemed to be ended. We were relaxing in peace, when a blow from the South, late in 1903, was the worst of all received until today. Let us describe it.

In July 1903, a notable Franciscan had disembarked at Smyrna and lodged for a while at St. Marie's, with his colleagues. His name? Father Barnabe. His origin? From Alsace, that means neither French nor German; but in mind more German than French. His Order? He was from the Custodianship of Jerusalem. His work? He was known in Palestine for his work upon Jerusalem and its neighbourhoods, numerous works widely appreciated. They reproached him for publishing too quickly, of abusing texts and conclusions, of spicing his opinions and style. He was, besides, an intelligent man, a hard worker, very inquiring; nobody contested his qualities.

What did he come to do at Smyrna? He came to study on the spot Panaghia and the Panaghia question.

He came to see me at Sacre-Coeur; we spoke. It was impossible to perceive his thoughts. Was he speaking about Panaghia? Nonsense words, insignificant or uncertain, and gloomy. Did I want to summarise his sayings? He escaped my questions, speaking about his work in Jerusalem. Finally, he told me about his wish to go up to Panaghia. "Very well, Father, go, it is a good opportunity. M. Jung is up there, he will be a host as well a guide".

On July 7, Thursday, together with M. Jung and M. Roussel, Rev. Barnabe set off for Panaghia, a companion with him. He wished to walk up there. The way is long, the ascent hard and rocky, the sun hot, very hot, and his habit was of thick baize, and he was wearing wooden sandals. Thus, they were very tired when they arrived at the House. Father Barnabe was in a bad mood. Meanwhile, he started a discussion while walking: "C. Emmerich says three hours", or "they made it in only two hours". M. Jung interrupted "Father, you are tired, take a rest, we will dine soon after, and later we will speak about whatever you want."

The Father came up to him. "Father," asked M. Jung, "have you been southwards to the bottom of the plain?" "No." "Have you climbed up the narrow paths through Kara-Kais, which leads to the terraces? Towards the mountain top?" "No." Then what are you talking about? C. Emmerich's way is not the way you have taken."

After dinner, we examined carefully and minutely the chapel and surroundings. Later, when the sun went down, we spoke about the Castle and terrace. M. Jung being hurt in his leg, M. Roussel proposed to guide him.

They had to climb up again via difficult paths under a sun still very hot. To finish, the Father hurt himself on the stones, he scratched himself on the brambles. One moment he was upbraiding M. Roussel, almost accusing him of leading him through the lost ways on purpose, as a joke. Mr. Roussel shouted angrily: "Who do you think I am?"

It needed very little to leave the two Fathers there and go home alone. Easy to understand, in such conditions it wasn't a question of going either to the terrace, or to Bulbul-Dagh's top from where Efesus and the sea could be seen, as C. Emmerich says. From the Castle we went down to the logia.

The Father understood his mistake and apologised to M. Roussel during supper; later he started his criticisms again.

"The chapel is not situated as they claim." It was M. Roussel who answered. "I am an ex-student of the Polytechnic School, and for the moment Chief-ingenue of the Smyrna-cassaba; I suppose I know about orientation, besides I have been almost twenty times to Panaghia and I have stayed for weeks. I assure you, my Reverend, the chapel is perfectly situated."

Things didn't go any further. Early next morning they hurried to get down to Efesus, to see the ruins. He left a troubled impression on M. Jung and M. Roussel.

On his return, he came to thank me. "So Father, are you satisfied with what you have seen?" "Yes, but it is not as I was thinking." "What did you suppose you would find? The house entire, as the Holy Virgin left it, as C. Emmerich described it? Do not forget Father, eighteen centuries have passed; it needs less to make ruins!" "Then I remarked on the wall stones, which are not old." "Of course. There are some dating back forty years, when Andrea rebuilt some fallen walls; there are also some we put there ourselves in recent years. But the important thing is the basement and also what remains from the primitive building." etc. etc.

I understood very well from his awkward language, his equivocal style, from his reticence above all, that there were other things that didn't satisfy him; but what? -"Let us see, Father," said I, plainly. "Do you have any objection? Difficulties to point out?" "Yes...No..." "Trifles which I didn't understand." "Here, Father," said I, to make him feel easy; "Take your time; and write down all that has shocked you or that you didn't appreciate".

Upon this, he bowed and left. I didn't see him again. Some days later I knew he had gone to Jerusalem, where he would prepare to blow up Panaghia and Panaghists!

In fact the explosion happened in November 1903, in the shape of a thick volume of 300 pages entitled: The Holy Virgin's Grave at Jerusalem. After having at first overrun Rome and all centres that seemed favourable to him with his book, Rev. Barnabe deigned to send us two copies: one for Mr. Jung one for me, as a consideration offered by the author. Thank you very much, Father Barnabe!

I read, and I was quite reassured for us. I recognised also that it was the most terrible war weapon that had been fired against Panaghia and the thesis of Panaghia. I was as reassured for us as I was frightened for the others.

It was not a clever book, that is why I was reassured for us. But it is a false and perfidious book. For that reason it is very dangerous. That is why I was frightened for others. Meaningless assertions, contradicting each other; negations without any consistency, particular or general conclusions; false or illogical reasoning; an accumulation of authorities without authorities; an accumulation of texts mutilated or amplified or distorted from their true sense, or suspicions, or irrelevant questions. In reality it is deficient, very deficient. It is enough to clarify it a little to demonstrate all the deep misery of the man's astuteness.

But it is as terrible in its appearance and machinery. The author affirms so surely; he denies so audaciously. He mixes with ability truth and falsity; he presents with so much assurance as good and indisputable a lot of testimonies that say nothing or are without any value. He gives so shamelessly for old and universal what is less universal and old, etc. etc. Except if you are in on the secret or the cause, as we are, it is almost impossible to perceive the imposture, far easier to be shocked, convinced by the book.

Who does he ask to check his texts? Who does he ask to identify testimonies? Who suspects the treachery of so many affirmations? Of so many audacious and ruinous negations? Who looks for the failure of the logic of such deductions, of such conclusions?

Who can separate the tares from the wheat? One reads without distrust and one is carried away. I am not astonished by Abbot Turmel's cry, after he had read Father Barnabe: "It is the end of Panaghia's legend!" ...or Monsignor Radin Tedeschi saying to Rev. Eschbach! "Do not we speak any more of Efesus." I am not astonished any more, he imprisoned other good spirits and dissuaded them from us. That is, I say, a dangerous book, very dangerous.

Composed of 320 pages, 12 chapters and parts. In the First part he states that the Holy virgin has never been to Efesus, nor in the neighbourhood. He tries to prove that by the scripture, by the Fathers, by tradition and his two visionaries: Saint Brigitte of Sweden, and Mary of Agreda. In the third part, he pretends there is no similarity between Panaghia and C. Emmerich's description the House is a Byzantine chapel later than the 4th century, looking more like a mosque of the 16th centruy than a gymnasium of the 1st century "Finally the, Kirkindji tradition is a fiction or a farce of their Mayor, Constantinidis."

We did not think at first to write or even less to publish a regular refutation against F. Barnabe's lucubrations. In fact, he republished old stories, but it was necessary that the good F. Barnabe understand that we didn't feel defeated. For this goal, I was amusing myself by scribbling down some thoughts, my pen running over about thirty pages, where, taking the pages one by one I demolished his principal arguments, even their bases with pleasure.

Before sending to F.Barnabe this manuscript reply, I sent a copy to Rev. Eschbach at Rome, He replied soon: "It is moved and moving, thrilled and thrilling but uncompleted..."He told me then the enormous impression F. Barnabe's pamphlet had made in the principal centres at Rome. He concluded: "A complete and regular refutation is needed." M. Lobry said the same.

It was a huge, huge task I had to do. Thank God I had read enough of F. Barnabe's book; the other side knew my subject very well, no reason to be anxious. But the frame of the work, the way to distinguish between truth and lies!... But the frame'? A frame to please everybody without hurting anybody. But the style!...without excess or pretension, while animated and firm, constrained sometimes to veil, while always clear; simple while varied enough to say fifty times the same thing without tiring the reader; plain while pleasing!. In nomine Domini! Amen;

Father Barnabe has taken as a title: The Holy Virgin's Grave at Jerusalem. His title inspired ours; the anti-Barnabe thrust was intitulated:

"The Holy Virgin's Grave at Efesus."

There were two parts in the work: in the first part we relieved with details F. Barnabe's contradictions, his manifested errors, his defective citations, his haphazard and proofless assertions, his worthless insinuations etc. etc.

There were as many subjects as there were particular articles. In the second part, we attacked the thesis; after that had been demolished, torn to pieces, we opposed it with our own thesis, with proofs, with just as many articles and as many theses.

This created a lot of questions (to which F. Barnabe was kindly asked to reply,) which all tended rationally to explode the Jerusalem tradition, to touch upon its weakness, its misery, also its ridiculous sides.

We made use of the occasion to inform readers in an epilogue with measure and reserve of new discoveries, recent finds, as well as healings miraculously attributed to Panaghia's ashes!

It needed time to put all this in order. Briefly, the manuscript ended in mid-June, 1904, and was sent at once to the printer.

Then a terror came over me; a strange terror! What abot all those who had read the manuscript, as they had in the course of the work. When it was completely ended, it would be sent to Paris, agreed with unanimity, firmly and neatly. Father Barnabe would be put down, without any remission. I myself was thinking the same as they did, went but even further than them... Ergo: F. Banabe had only one solution to save himself; to stop Anti Barnabe from appearing. How? Index? Index? Yes, Index; I was not the only one to feel such a fear. They are so powerful in Rome; the Capuchins, Franciscans and all of them are cunning enough to manage the "offices". Had we not had a similar case at Smyrna? The innocent life of St. Polycarpe published by the Abbot Octave Mirzan with the Clergy's and believer's subscriptions, with approbation and signature of the Archbishop. For one word-in fact true- but not well-accepted by the "neuvenairs", the very kind Father Bernardine had succeeded in having the book put in "Index".

We might escape -if need presented- from a similar plot. In consequence, I wrote first to Oudin: "Your first sending must be to Rome; the others later." In the same way I wrote to Rev. Eschbach, I told him my fear. I informed him of the sending of 150-200 copies of the new booklet, asking urgently of him to send them everywhere: to Cardinals, chiefs of Orders, Prelates, notabilities etc. etc. et quam primum. I was quite sure, the booklet being in the hands of all the Most Eminents, the Most Learned that I had no reason to fear Barnabe's machinery.

Thus said, thus done. On 7th November, Rev. Eschbach wrote to me from Rome: "When you receive the present, the spiritual and terrible Gabrielovich will be the guest of all the Most Eminent Cardinals and principal high prelates of the Eternal

City, already it is half done. For two days the postal packets have been arriving: distribution has started at once. The book is in the Cardinals' hands: Farewell, Censure." "Besides," Rev. Eschbach reassured me; "About the Index," continued in the same letter "The pious Gabrielovich can be without any fear. We agree he acted with wisdom, and best, he succeeded in giving nothing for Censure.

I could sleep quite peacefully, waiting for the booklet's effect. Besides, I had hope first in the "Sweet Virgin" who had inspired me to write the booklet, also in the circumstances, which have been favourable. We were on the eve of the Marial Congress., Leading lights ran from everywhere to the Eternal City. The moment "Mary's Grave at Efesus" appeared in Rome: this learned, curious, pious centre received the AntiBarnabe booklet.

After the second day, Rev. Eschbach wrote to me about our booklet's affect on Rome: "Some of the readers admitted the booklet amused them, because of the notice to the reader before the epilogue. They even failed to feel charity innocently, of course, laughing loudly to the detriment of the poor F. Barnabe. Other readers, cool tempered, observed it was a good work, with much serious research; it would make an impression on our modern critics. "As for me," continues Rev. Eschach; "I agree with the two groups of readers, I shall add- under my sleeve- my humble idea. Here Gabrielovich has surpassed himself. Tell him, simply and well, I will not darken his horizon."

An encouraging beginning! Later Rome will give us better. We will come again. What did they say at Jerusalem? After Rome, it is the most important centre for the question. I have three letters from Jerusalem. The impression created by Anti-Barnabe, on the learned and cosmopolitan world of the Holy City,

1) From the Rev. Verdier, free priest, ex-student of M. Ulysse Chevalier, Jerusalem, 13 January 1905.

"I applaud and say: Bravo! You destroy by your replies the authority of this man, who, to defend a cause, uses all means. He took against him a resolute adversary of the French Community, himself French, and some of the sanctuaries they possess at Jerusalem.

After the decisive replies and execution you impose on him, he is now disregarded. Thank you on behalf of our Communities, so persecuted by him and his fellows. If there remains some modesty in him, he should keep silent from now on."

2) From Rev. Coulbeaux, former chief of our Mission in Abyssinia, after Mons, Crouzet, today resident in Jerusalem.

Jerusalem, 21 March 1905

"Where are they after your reply?...."

"General, universal satisfaction for the annihilation of Rev. Barnabe. F. Barnabe felt crushed after so many blows Nothing was spared -he would say- neither the subject, nor the shape. Conversions? None! It does not come so quickly...some cannot come back to reason where is no reason...In fact "there is no reason to shrug ones shoulders anymore, to compress salivating lips with this word: "It is nonsense." Patience and perseverance on your work."

3) From Monsignor Vivien, Doctor of Theology, former Great Vicar of Chambery, former Parish of Saint-Louis of France in Moscow, Privy Chamberlain of His Holiness, now retired at Notre-Dame-de France.

Jerusalem, 7January 1905

"...Your Mary's Grave at Efesus reconciled me with the idea, Jerusalem is not set up on testimonies as authentic as its revindications, as those of C.Emmerich's testimonies.

As for Barnabe, nothing was said about his impressions. But all that was said in my neighbourhood was: the blow administered to him must be disconcerting for him as well as pleasant, for the public is long tired of his impertinence, presumption and the pride of this "humble" son of St. Francis d'Assisi." At the same time you broke the dominant sceptre of the terrible critic, an article of Evhos of Orient and inflicted a blow that was even less but also palpable, a "dig" against his Caiphe Palace...written not in Caipha's honour but in hate against the Assumptionists... F. Jaquemin has set him well in the pillory of the impostor for whom nothing is true except what is advantageous to him etc...

The same from a Canon from Sens. "You speak to me, dear Reverend, about the Holy Virgin's Grave at Efesus. Gabrielovich's book is here on my table, open at page 159. I must say it made a great sensation in Jerusalem, not only because he crushes F. Barnabe, (who crushed everybody as well) with the intensity of his arguments. Maybe one could reproach him for his fiery tone. He did not need it considering his proof against F. Barnabe's claims. I do not deny It the work is huge. It will open through contemporary opinion an easy way to Efesus revindications.

"Gabrielovich to Catherine Emmerich has done, since now her name can be pronounced everywhere without blushing or smiling".

Jerusalem, 30 December 1904

From France the same. Father Ollivier, the great Dominican orator, appreciates the work with one word: "it is a masterpiece."

Reverend Fiat, who after reading the book took it triumphantly to Dax, to the man he knew was the most sceptical against Panaghia and Efesus.

" Do read it Rev. Cartel, read it" And Rev. Cartel, after he had read it, said in his turn: "I have started to believe."

The Rev. Moyse from Orleans, as we already know, writes from Lyons on 6 November 1904; "Let me thank you for your "Holy Virgin's Grave at Efesus", first because I owe your copy to your kind charity, and also whose reading gave me so much pleasure.

"Ah, how happy I was to see demolished the pamphlet of this poor Barnabe, where the pedant reached the summit of impudence, of discourtesy and even more, it seems, of disloyalty".

"You have used the sword with velvet gloves; but it did not stop the blows from falling, and if the fellow's skin is tattooed, he merited it."

"Some months ago, F. Barnabe's booklet was sent to me by one of our religious at Constantinople. I read it with affliction, at moments, I confess, with fury, and I wished with ardour to see you defend yourself one day. You have done it magisterially. I take the respectful freedom to congratulate you, and I bless with all my soul the Good Lord and Holy Virgin."

Rome, at last, will give in the Pope's name the last note, through the Cardinal, State Secretary.

Rome, Folio 11026

Most Reverend,

It is with particular pleasure that the Holy Father received the three opuscules published by the Most Illustrious Segniory with the goal of bringing new light to the difficult problem of the place of death and the Assumption of the Most Holy Virgin. His Holiness noticed with satisfaction all the force of the investigations done on this serious subject by your Signory and Colleagues. Thus, thanking especially Your Signory for the pleasant gift, His Holiness declares Himself grateful also to the other priests of the Mission of Smyrna, according to you and also to these Reverends the Apostolic Blessing. He prays to the

Good Lord and His August Mother to bestow always more and more abundances, the divine light, to all those who, with filial tenderness, consecrate their studies to search for the place where Mary's Grave is concealed.

"Expressing also, for all my gratitude for the same copies you sent me so courteously, I assure you of my feelings of high esteem.

Of V.S.R.
In God's Love
R. Card. Merry del Val.
Rome, 5 April 1905

To Rev. Eug. Poulin, Priest of the Mission, Superior of the College of Sacre-Coeur, Smyrna.

This letter is so good, it so encourages the Chief of the Church, it encouraged the Discoverers of Panaghia, and accentuated the affect already produced.

Reverend Fiat wrote to from the Main House:

Paris, 25 April 1905

"I congratulate you for the Holy Father's good and encouraging letter sent to you. This is enough to compensate you for the attacks you have received. It seems to me your thesis is good and contrary arguments do not nullify it. If it was permitted to use hunter's language, I should say you are the footprints to follow with constancy and trust. You will reach, in a while, your goal of establishing definitely the fact of the Holy Virgin's death at Efesus."

Monsignor Vivien wrote to me again from Jerusalem on 3 May 1905.

"May God send you signs, calls, indications with his finger. Of course, God's finger gave you precious indications; that which seemed impossible ten years ago to the public, has became so avowable, so worthy of investigation, so solicited that the unbelievers, the fun-makers of yesterday, have today opened their eyes to you, to survey every new trace, you will have the luck to discover. People are sincerely happy at every new light which gives to your investigations hope nearest to your success. The others are enraged to see so soon their oppositions driven back and disproved. Waiting for the hour of triumph, I have established with warm interest the cutting down of all bushes, the levelling of all the paths, the escarpments which made the way tortuous, zigzagging and unbearable removed."

"The kind Father Coulbeaux showed me Rome's reply to your Homeric fight against F. Barnabe from Alsace, it is extremely encouraging. One can see him saying: "I am with you.""

"It seems to me that the increasing repugnance against F. Barnabe has become a heaven of sympathy for you and your thesis. In any case this matador who went to Efesus to give the last stroke to Efesian hopes, is now so piteous, so broken down, that his broken condition adds to our case previous success and permits us to hope that more is possible".

The same the "Revue du Clerge," before against us, is now apologising. On 1 July 1904, after reading F. Barnebes volume, Rev. Abbot Turmel, forgetting that before he had pronounced it was necessary to listen to both sides, has written thoughtlessly in "Revue du Clerge": "Finish with Panaghia's legend." Then wrote this little letter as follows:

Smyrna, 8 July 1904

Dear Reverend Abbot,

Your kind faith has been surprised, as of many others, by the more peremptory than exact and sure affirmations of the kind Father Barnabe. I know that the reply is ready and that the reply will soon be published. I hope, after reading this reply, you will think like us, and that there will be beautiful and good days to live for Panaghia-Capouli. Will you please etc. etc....

When the Anti-Barnabe appeared, I sent a copy to the Abbot Turmel. He read it and saw the truth. "It must be said that after the Holy Virgin's Grave at Efesus nothing remains for F. Barnabe, nor the Holy Virgin's Grave at Jerusalem."

It would be very simple to give up so quickly, some reflections like Parthe's arrows against Efesus tradition still followed.

I replied with the following note:

Smyrna, 8 March 1905

Reverend Abbot,

Five or six years ago, Rev. Camus, today Monsignor Le Camus, Bishop of de la Rochelle, was in transit through Smyrna accompanied by the learned and modest Rev. Vigoroux. Rev. Camus was joking: "I don't believe in Jerusalem, nor even in Efesus." "Very well," said one of his interlocutors: "Let us say H.V. died at Mecca, and we will not speak about it any more."

With your two articles about the Holy Virgin's grave you reach the same end.

Practically, the fact is simple. There are only two traditions in the world: Jerusalem or Efesus, if not Jerusalem, then Efesus. All this is dilemma, Reverend Abbot. I have the honour etc. etc...

When the 'Holy Virgin's Grave at Efesus' appeared, it was catalogued in Paris, in Rev. Vigouroux's great Biblical Dictionary. Rev. Lesetre, one of the great parishes of Paris, was in charge of this work. Involved in his previous studies and his own ideas, Rev. Lesetre, who didn't attach any importance to the new work, concluded that nothing was for Jerusalem and against Efesus. This did not stop him from showing as a reference, at the end of the article, the Grave at Efesus, which he has not even read. It was unlucky the Rev. Vigouroux was not there. Things would have been otherwise but unfortunately Rev. Vigouroux was in Rome for the Marial Congress. We knew from himself that he regretted Rev. Lesetre's conclusion. Once he intervened for the Efesus article, he had to cancel a whole thesis against Efesus. He hoped to retake the article about Mary; but they profited from his being absent to conclude without him.

I made it my duty to protest, so I addressed a letter to Rev. Lesetre himself.

Smyrna, 30 December 1904

Reverend Parish,

Would you please permit me on the occasion of your article on Mary, three small questions or observations, as it is said?

1) You designate Abul-faradj, of the 13th century, as the first to speak about the stay and death of Holy Mary at Efesus. Is there not anyone before Abul-Faradj, at least for the stay, Hippolite the Theban of the 10th century? (-see Dic. Patr. de Mign, III, p. 338.) -And before Hippolite the Theban, Notker, (9th centtury), who gives the two opinions? And before Notker, Helecca from Saragossa, (8th century) -V.Bivarious sur Flavius Dexter. And before Helecca, the tradition of Moun Athos, which claims the Holy Virgin herself founded the first nunnery of Athos during a journey she made when she dwelt at Efesus?

2) It is true that St. Epiphany, really doubted the Holy Virgin's death; and he did not say so, because there was nothing exactly known about her death, also about her sepulchre?

Whatever man's personal opinion could be, there is in 'Father's word an historic and testified fact. The pious and learned Father had never known Mary's Grave at Jerusalem: Quippe haud scican de SSma acBBma Virgine obscura quaedam inveniri possint vestigia, quae incertam nobili illius mortis Eidem faciant. Haeres. 78 The pious and learned Father has no knowledge about Jerusalem's tradition vestigia etiam oscura. - The pious and learned Father certifies that nobody know more; necsimus. It is written at length; nobody of his contemporaries contests it. Beside this authentic, historical, formal testimony, the unanimous silence of all the Bishops, of all the pilgrims of Jerusalem, for more than four centuries confirm and support it.

On which serious basis do you prefer to accord more trust to three apocryphers, condemned by Pope Gelase, than to the testimony so solid and clear of S. Epiphany? The testimony is indirect but very neat, concluded by the silence of all the authors and contemporary historians.

3) You say authentic documents are missing for Efesus. Is it true? Let us go. Which are the authentic documents for Jerusalem? To what does Jerusalem refer her whole tradition? Except the apocryphers?

I remain etc....

It is eighteen months since Mary's Grave at Efesus appeared to the public; there has not been any voice, anything written against it. The opposition put its hand upon its mouth and shut up; even those who had not disarmed, controlled their anger. That is something.

In Germany converts of C. Emmerich, the Abbot Niessen, Chaplain of St. Adalbert, Aix-la-Chapelle became the courageous champions of Panaghia and Efesus. We are in correspondence and united for the common cause.

Last year 1906, Rev. Niessen, in agreement with us, published all our theses in German enriched by all the new documents he could procure, with new comments he had made. There has been approval, from everyone, from Protestants as well as from Catholics.

All agreed to recognise there is no basis in the apocryphers, nor Juvenal, nor the Euthimian Historical which is of the 9th century. All, or almost all, agree to recognise, that since 350 (the fourth century), the Efesus tradition has existed. As for Jerusalem, there is nothing before 600. Finally, everyone recognises Jerusalem's tradition referred to only by the apocryphers. No word from the Pseudo Denys, from Nirsh about all these reports; only to laugh at the efforts of the kind Learned men looking for something valorous for the said Pseudo Denys.

Of the varions testimonies collected by Rev. Niessen about his book, I retained only three:

The first is the judgement about the Stones of Holy Cross Way, by the Learned Carl Mack, Savant professor Orientalist from Siebourg, "...Concerning the pieces of the Stations so interesting for me, I think the characteristics are surely Hebrew and of the first century A.D Some of these characteristics remind us, by their form, of those found on the old coins. On the first stone I read -id est MZB, it means 'Madzab". It is a word very often met on Punic funeral monuments, that which in Hebrew means: station.

We are in the presence of punic Hebrew inscriptions. How from the Punic and Hebrew could they have moved to a centre so Greek if it is not as C.Emmerich explains.

The second testimony is that of the learned and famous Otto Bardenhewer, professor at the Catholic University at Münich, a great admirer of the Visionary of Dülmen. He avoids the question of the Discovery, but he accords the four following points, so important:

1) The testimonies of Jerusalem all derive from the apocryphers.

2) St. Epiphany testifies to an Efesus traditon; it is arbitrary that they want to present a testimony for Jerusalem. Besides

he is a man of this country, who very often does not know about the death and grave of the Holy Virgin.

3) Eutimienny historically dates from the 9th century. (it is an interpolation in the text of St. John Damascene)

4) The Efesus Council is the main proof for Efesus. The third proof is different, but also precious. It is a letter from Cardinal Steinhuber to Rev. Niessen, as a respectable reply to his book.

Rome, 17 September 1906

"I gave the Holy Father the copy you addressed to him.

His Holiness accepted it with an ardent interest, saying He shared your opinion, above all because of these words: Accepit cam in sua.

He will send you a brief. All I read in your book left me the best impression. The demonstration given to the first part, Jerusalem's legend, and the II. Efesus Tradition seems very successful. As for the III. Panaghia-Capouli, a definitive judgement would be possible when the Congregation of the Rites is pronounced. In any case, the Work is well appreciated for its sureness of judgement, its precise certitude, also the author's ability.

Signed: A. Card. Steinhuber

That proves conclusively by these appreciations the accomplished work done in Germany, in all minds, concerning Panaghia Capouli and our thesis. It is a discreet remark that any observer could have made on the occasion of a recent appeal addressed to the Catholic Women of Germany, as a favour to the famous German Church of Mont Sion. Here is the beginning and principal part: "The Dormition, this place we Catholics owe to the good will of His majesty the Emperor William II. It is particularly venerable for Catholic women. Very near the Cenacle rises where it has been instituted.

The Sacrament of Eucocrist.Here the first holy women lived in the days following the Lord's Ascension, praying together with the Apostles. They had been testimonies of the Holy Spirit's Descent, and also those who received His Divine Gift. The Dormition is the place where women's apostolic activity in the new Church arose. There, at John's house, the first Christian women gathered around Mary with their prayers and repeated the Apostle's sayings. It was at Sion that they learned the dignity of the apostleship from God's Mother. Following in their footsteps walked a great number of noble girls who still follow the Mission, rich in graces, to give the eternal light to the world. The Apostolic Union of Catholic German Women...etc" The rest has not any connection with our subject.

Do you notice?...The church at Sion, all that interest and piety make one like the work. There is no word, neither the death nor the Holy Virgin's Assumption, except for the word Dormition, repeated twice, as a very simple appellative known in the place concerned.

Is it not suggestive? In Germany they deny Jerusalem's legend, they have begun to believe that even if the Holy Virgin remained at Sion for a while, it was not there that she finished her life. Let us note this remark, it is a good sign. And now, after all these publications, all these arguments, where are we?

We establish an Efesus tradition so abandoned, so disparaged fifty years ago, but one which occupied its place in public opinion, a good and beautiful place. Let us establish Jerusalem's tradition, once so proud, so unkind towards these poor "discoverers", now modest, very modest after the terrible thump it received and it is reduced today to defending itself. Let us establish everywhere, in France, Italy, Spain, Germany, Constantinople, Smyrna even Jerusalem that a great sudden change has take place in Efesus-Jerusalem opinion.

Let us establish that Rome inclines towards us. For us in the past was Benedictus XIV and the practice of previous centuries. For us in the present are Roman Ordo, huge numbers of dignitaries. Among the principal ones are Cardinal Prefect of Rites, Aloysi Masella, Cardinal Vicar of Rome, His Excellency Parochi.

For us above all is Pope Pius X, shares our opinion, Cardinal Steinhuber, too.

Let us establish that Panaghia rises, rises, and becomes greater every year, and that Jerusalem falls, falls and decreases more and more.

It is a victory? Definitive triumph? No, not yet, all this announces a victory, a triumph that will come and is not far away.

Fourteen years, ago in the letter of March 1893, to Rev. Allou, Congregation's Assistant we said: the stone has been detached from the mountain and it is rolling.

It will roll, and no human hand will be able to stop it rolling. "At Domino..... Today after the events we accomplished we can add to the word of the first hour: A Domino....... Nostris, and the rest of the verse: Et est..... a prediction has been accomplished, marvellously; our eyes are the witnesses.

To God who has inspired and led us. To Mary, who encouraged and blessed us glory, honour, gratitude Love... Amen.

As for the poor workers who were associated with Divine Work and maybe retarded it because of their ignorance, impeded it because of their neglect, spoiled it by their errors, grant them pardon and also a pious prayer.

18 March 1908
Celebration of Saint Gabriel

Pilgrimage to Efesus with Monsignor Roncalli; later Pope John XXIII, 25/06/1931, for the 1500th anniversary of the Council at Efesus.

Visit of Pope Paul VI on 26/07/1967

Mons. André P. Timoni 1879-1904
Archibishop of Smyrna, days of discovery.

Views of Holy Virgin's House, days of discovery.

Holy Cross Way. Rev. Jung and Sister Mandat de Grancey.

Sister Marie de Mandat Grancey (+1915)

First visitors with guardian's family.

M. H. Jung, Lazariste

First post-card of
the Holy Virgin.

Gravure of the house, by P. d'Andria 1896.

Gravure by Raymond Péré (August 1898)

Architect of the Horloge Tower at Smyrna, and painter of the frescos of the church St. Polycarpe.

A

PANAGHIÂ-CAPOULI.

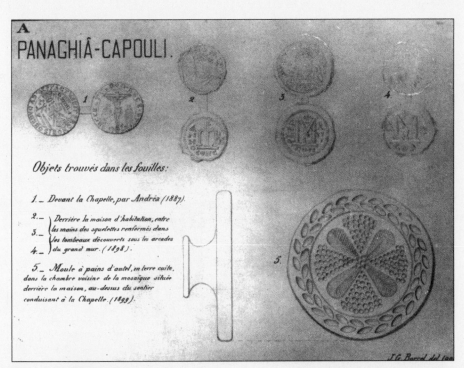

Objets trouvés dans les fouilles:

1.— Devant la Chapelle, par Andréa (1887).

2.— ⎫ *Derrière la maison d'habitation, entre*
3.— ⎬ *les mains des squelettes renfermés dans*
       ⎪ *les tombeaux découverts sous les arcades*
4.— ⎭ *du grand mur. (1898).*

5.— Moule à pains d'autel, en terre cuite,
dans la chambre voisine de la mosaïque située
derrière la maison, au-dessus du sentier
conduisant à la Chapelle. (1899).

J.G. Borrel del. 190.

B

PANAGHIA-CAPOULI.

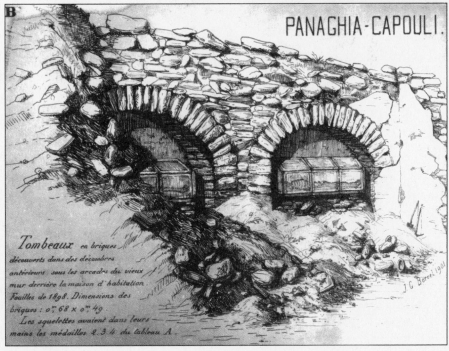

Tombeaux en briques
découverts dans des décombres
antérieurs sous les arcades du vieux
mur derrière la maison d'habitation.
Fouilles de 1898. Dimensions des
briques: 0ᵐ 68 × 0ᵐ 49.
Les squelettes avaient dans leurs
mains les médailles 2.3.4 du tableau A.

J.G. Borrel 1901

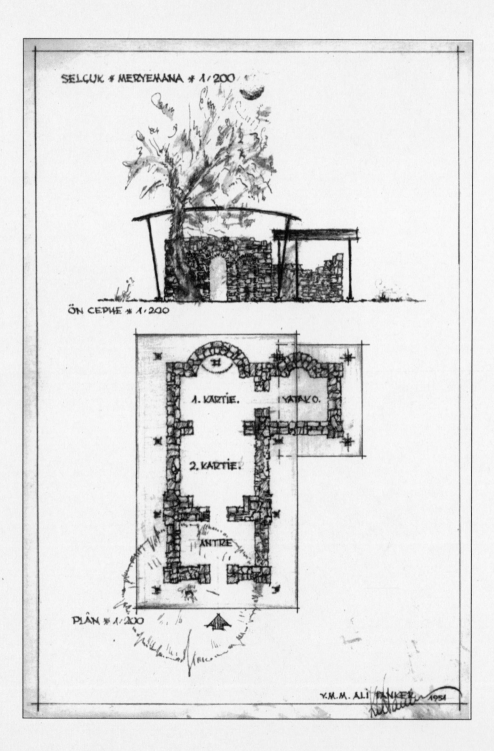

SELÇUK ∦ MERYEMANA ∦ 1/200

ÖN CEPHE ∦ 1/200

1. KARTIE.   YATAKO.

2. KARTIE.

ANTRE

PLÂN ∦ 1/200

Y.M.M. ALI PANKER 1951